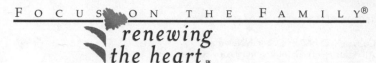

FOCUS ON THE FAMILY®
*renewing
the heart*™

then God created Woman

Finding Fulfillment as the Woman God Intended You to Be

Dr. Deborah Newman

Tyndale House Publishers, Wheaton, Illinois

THEN GOD CREATED WOMAN

ISBN 1-56179-533-X

A Focus on the Family Book Published by
Tyndale House Publishers, Wheaton, Illinois 60189

The case examples presented in this book are fictional composites based on the author's clinical experience with hundreds of clients through the years. Any resemblance between these fictional characters and actual persons is coincidental.

Focus on the Family books are available at special quantity discounts when purchased in bulk by corporations, organizations, churches, or groups. Special imprints, messages, and excerpts can be produced to meet your needs. For more information, contact: Sales Dept., Focus on the Family, 8605 Explorer Drive, Colorado Springs, CO 80920; or phone (719) 531-3400.

Editor: Michele A. Kendall
Cover Design: Candi Park D'Agnese
Cover Photo: Color Box / FPG International

Printed in the United States of America
98 99 00 01 02 03 / 10 9 8 7 6 5

To Brian

With love, admiration, and appreciation

Contents

Acknowledgments

First I would like to thank God for the message of this book, that we are His precious creation, His beloved daughters. I also would like to acknowledge the prayers, support, and encouragement of my prayer group: Janet, Freda, Brenda, Robin, Deborah, Vicki, Patricia, Trina, and Jennifer. Deborah Russell was kind enough to proofread the manuscript, baby-sit my children, and do anything else I needed. Thank you, Deborah.

I would also like to express my appreciation to Focus on the Family Book Publishing, particularly Gwen Ellis, former managing editor, for getting this project started, and Michele Kendall, book editor, for seeing the project through to the end. Your insights and encouragement have been invaluable. I'm grateful to Mike Leming and the marketing department for their creative influence. Sandy Dengler—friend, mentor, and talented writer—read through the entire manuscript and helped me to clearly communicate my thoughts.

Finally, to my husband, Brian, and my children, Rachel and Benjamin: You have been wonderful through this whole process. Thank you for your love, support, and sacrifices.

$\mathcal{D}$iscovering True Feminine Identity

R ecently, I became intrigued by a song I heard. It was a ballad mocking the infamous fairy tale about Cinderella. Cinderella was addressed as a real woman who had led many others astray by promising them through her example that once they found their Prince Charming, they would live happily ever after. The singer scornfully asked her if the shoe still fit and challenged her to explain why she had been able to dupe so many women.

This singer is not alone in her attitude. Almost every woman has asked herself similar questions. Whether the springboard is Cinderella-like stories, the Bible, feminism, or something else, somehow all the promises women receive don't seem to fit with reality.

Most women accept the subtle messages the world tells us about what we need to be as women—young, sexy, rich, powerful. Others of us try to measure ourselves by certain roles we see outlined in the Bible—submissive, gentle, hospitable. But there is so much more God wants us to experience as women. With this book, I hope to provide you

1

with an anchor for your soul that helps steady you against the world's empty claims to femininity. As you realize where you've placed your false sense of security, you will discover that as a woman, you have unique struggles in this world and your problems have unique answers.

What is the secret to unmasking your true feminine identity? Through the years, as I've come to see myself more accurately, I've discovered that there are three areas we must explore on our journey to unmasking and claiming our true feminine identity.

1. We Need to Understand What Makes Us Tick as Women

Women were created differently from men. Women were cursed differently from men. Truthfully, if we tried to decipher every difference between men and women, we would probably count into the hundreds. When we accept and embrace these differences, we can figure out how we best fit in this world.

Women's problems with identity, security, purpose, and direction all lead back to our sense of relational well-being—how secure and contented we feel about the people closest to us. Think about the biggest problem you have in your life right now. I can almost guarantee you that the central factor in that problem somehow involves relationships.

God gives women unique information about how He created us and basically what makes us tick. When we discover why relationships are so central to how we view ourselves as women, we are freed up by a better understanding of who we are.

2. We Need to Identify the Obstacles That Prevent Us from Seeing What Great Women We Are

Most of us are confused, unsatisfied, and searching for a sense of identity because we don't recognize who we really are. Reading Ephesians 1–3, Psalm 139, or the many scriptures in which God gives us an awesome picture of our identity as believers in Christ usually doesn't change our stubborn sense of worthlessness. What we will discover is that the souls of women are not made of Teflon. Rejection sticks to them like greasy grime to a steel pot. What makes us tick as women is our relationships, and when we've been wounded in a relationship, it will definitely distort how we view ourselves and how valuable we think we are to the world we live in.

3. We Need to Develop a More Intimate Relationship with God

Healing these wounds in our relationships prepares our hearts to experience a relationship with God as never before. Saint Augustine said, "Because you have made us for yourself, our hearts are restless until they rest in You."[1] The true rest for our souls, the nourishment we have been seeking from the world, is within reach. We don't have to climb Mount Everest or journey to a rain forest to find this precious commodity. By opening our hearts to God in a deeper way, we can discover His peace, a peace that takes away the anxiety and unrest that plague our sense of feminine identity.

These three areas provide the outline for this book. In Part One, we begin by discovering what makes women tick. In Part Two, we expose the obstacles to achieving a healthy feminine identity. Finally, in Part Three, we discover that the source of a true feminine identity is found in a love relationship with God. He longs to show us who we are and why we are here. The journey will lead us to the fresh water and green pastures for which our souls are longing. Come discover your unique design and the special beauty you possess as a woman.

PART ONE

What Makes Women Tick?

$\mathscr{A}$ Gathering of Women

What a grinding struggle Regina endured in trying to understand where she fit in the world. She tried so many roles, some consciously and some not, and every one of them disappointed her. Several nearly ruined her. Every woman explores to an extent, but Regina's whole life seemed to be a constant, fruitless experiment.

As a child she played the obedient eldest daughter role to perfection, being everything her parents seemed to want her to be. She went to church, made good grades, dated nice boys. But it didn't keep her father from leaving her mother. When her father left, something inside Regina seemed to wither. She determined that obeying the rules, dotting all the i's and crossing all the t's, avails a woman nothing.

Next she tried the newly emerging feminism role. Gleefully, she tossed aside all the moral baggage of her past and obeyed the new feminist dictum: Being a woman means being in control, fitting into no man's expectations, and equaling all that men are.

Then Regina encountered Christ. A new believer at 25, she looked to the church for answers about how to understand herself as a woman. Once in the church, Regina still lacked a sense of security. She had many questions that had no easy answers. At first she defined herself by a role she thought God wanted her to play. She studied all the scriptures that addressed what women should be. Quiet and gentle didn't fit with her gregarious personality, but if that was what God wanted, then she determined that that was what she would be.

Her journey toward happiness and wholeness took a new turn when at last she became totally frustrated and confessed her confusion and disappointment to two special women. They showed her how some of the wounds she carried were giving her a distorted picture of her value and purpose. With the help of these two friends, Regina was liberated to a point of finally embracing her womanhood in a new way. Now she hoped to help other women find this same freedom. She wanted to see them find answers to the two most important questions in life: (1) Who am I? and (2) Why am I here? She saw women being driven by these unanswered, and often subconscious, questions in almost everything they did.

For several years, Regina informally encouraged women as her mentors had encouraged her. But one year, God led her to begin a growth group in which members would focus on discovering, celebrating, and living their uniqueness as women in the body of Christ. The group met weekly to talk about life, God, and the Bible; to ask questions; and to receive encouragement. God put the names of several women on Regina's heart. Some of the women she knew well; others were just acquaintances. Regina had learned not to resist God's leading, so she didn't fret over how these women of different ages, classes, and spiritual maturity would mix. She just made the calls and invited the women into her home for a six-month growth and accountability group. Not surprising to Regina, who knew that God is in charge of it all, each of the six women was able to come.

That's why Judy, Sharon, Joy, Diane, Brenda, and Faye were all sitting on Regina's patio, laughing, chatting, and drinking coffee as the just-departed sun spread its last purple brush stroke across the western sky. Though strangers in many ways, these women were about to become instruments of God's grace in helping each other realize how God saw them and what He wanted for their lives.

JUDY: A shy, 23-year-old graduate student. As a child, she had been sexually abused by her father and brother. She had suicidal tendencies and was in counseling for major depression. In the previous year, she had finally received Christ as her Savior. Regina met Judy at church when Regina was speaking to the singles' group about how God made woman.

SHARON: A boisterous, 40-something, hard-working mother. After 17 years of marriage, she had separated from her husband, Ed, and she had recently discovered that her daughter was bulimic. Sharon was critical, angry, and disillusioned with God and the church. She was a longtime friend of Regina's.

JOY: A 50-something former beauty queen. She was always dressed like a model. She looked much younger than 50, and she never admitted her age. She was married and had two daughters. She had known Regina for years.

DIANE: A 33-year-old lawyer and divorced mother of two young children. She joined the group after confessing to the children's minister that she didn't know how her children were feeling about her recent divorce. The children's minister referred her to Regina, who invited her to the group.

BRENDA: A 39-year-old single woman who was the director of marketing for a large corporation. She worked with Regina on a community project, and Regina shared Christ with her and invited her to this group.

FAYE: A 40-year-old woman who had been married for 20 years. She had three children. She color-coded her monthly calendar to help her remember when to be where in order to meet all of her obligations. She cochaired the community event at which Brenda and Regina met.

When Regina invited these women into her home, she was really inviting them into her life. Regina was that kind of woman. She was so much at peace with herself that she wasn't ashamed to be caught off guard. She was bold enough to run into the grocery store without her makeup and dressed in her grubbiest clothes. She didn't even apologize for it when she ran into a friend. She just interacted with her friend as she would if she looked like a million bucks. After a conversation with Regina, you wanted to be like her. It wasn't that you envied her clothes, money, or hairstyle. You envied her peace. She had a sense of calm surrender. She never seemed uptight or frazzled.

Regina knew that other women envied her. They thought Regina was somehow more special to God because He had made her life so wonderful. To dispel those myths, she began by sharing her own life story with the group. She revealed how she had gotten to this place of peace and security. It was a tough journey, and it wasn't "happily ever after." You might be shocked that a woman with a past like Regina's could have become who she was today.

Regina's Story

Regina introduced herself as basically a product of the '60s. She grew up in a religious home. Her mother saw to it that the children went to church, and Regina was confirmed when she was 12 years old. From an early age, she was aware of her father's aloofness, and she never liked it that her father, so distant from the family, still held the power to make all the major decisions. The choice to divorce was the only decision Regina could recall her mother making, and Regina considered it the wrong one. When she got to college, Regina quickly shed her Goody Two-shoes image and experimented with ways to forge a better life for herself than the one offered by the suburbia that had trapped her mother.

During college, Regina was challenged by feminist thought. She was sure that feminism would rescue her from her sense of worthlessness as a woman. She thought she'd found the route to happiness—a route that fortuitously included drugs, uncommitted sex, and fun, none of which her mother had tasted except for the prescription Valium she took. Regina's college years were a blur of parties, protests, and pot.

After college, her friends became history, and that same old disillusionment again swept over Regina. In desperation, she accepted a coworker's invitation to a church meeting. For the first time, Regina opened her heart to God. But that wasn't the end of her pain.

A life dedicated to drugs, sex, and parties had left its scars, and perhaps none was as painful as her two abortions. A few months after she began a relationship with God, a group came to her new church. They said they were "pro-life," and they showed a film about abortion. It was all Regina could do to hold herself together. She left in the middle of the presentation to take refuge in the women's rest room. Alone with her sorrow, she wept bitterly. Pain, shame, and hopelessness overwhelmed her.

Suddenly, she felt someone touch her shoulder. Raising her eyes, she saw the pastor's wife, Louise, looking at her with concern.

Oh no! Regina thought. *I can't tell her why I'm crying! What am I going to do?*

Amazingly, Louise didn't say a word. She simply embraced Regina until her tears abated.

Then she said, "Regina, nothing you've ever done can separate you from the love of God."

"You don't understand. That film—they say I killed my two little babies."

Louise nodded. "But did you know that at the time? Regina, the world told you it was OK to kill those babies. The world blinded you from realizing what was really happening by telling you that a fetus is just a blob of tissue. You know the truth now. You didn't then. But even if you did, having an abortion cannot separate you from God's love."

Regina didn't believe Louise at first. But through reading the Bible, praying regularly with Louise, and working through the steps of grief, she finally came to accept that God truly loved her and forgave her for everything.

For the women gathered on her patio, Regina then summarized how what had happened in her life began the true healing of her femininity. Two years after she let God into her heart by believing that Jesus did die and rise again to cover her sins, she was baptized. She had waited because the abortion film she saw had shaken her faith; she needed time for the dust to settle, time to let her faith reform, time to think. Most of all, she resisted adding another meaningless ceremony to her religious experiences. She'd had enough of them as a child.

The day of her baptism was special for more than one reason. Not only was it the first day of her dedicated life, but it was also the first day she laid eyes on her future husband, Mike. Regina and Mike dated for two years and were married in the church where they met. For four years, they both worked. Then, after the birth of their first child, Regina quit her job. She felt this was the appropriate "Christian" thing to do. That decision created another crisis in Regina's spiritual life.

For Regina, being a Christian, acknowledging that abortion is a sin, and even getting married were radical departures from the beliefs she had adopted in college. She thought that a woman should "have it all." This meant that if a woman became pregnant, she should first consider whether it was the right time in her career or life to have a child before she decided to continue the pregnancy. She also believed a woman should never depend completely on a man for financial well-being. Secretly, she wondered whether some of the feminist views might be true, whether the Bible was a book that put women in their place. Staying at home to raise children seemed to trigger a deep fear that she would succumb to her mother's sterile life.

In the midst of this spiritual crisis, Mike received a promotion and was transferred to the city where they now lived and where their three children grew up. Regina was snatched, it seemed, from the spiritual nurturing and care she had come to rely on with Louise and the rest of her church.

Mike was little help during that time. He was so busy with his new job and adjusting to a new city that he hardly understood the struggle Regina was facing. Besides, he had not developed the deep relationships in their old church that Regina had.

Through those desperate days, God provided Regina with the friendship of two wonderful women: Hannah and Mary Ellen. Most of the women on the patio recognized the names as women who meant a lot to the people in their church. Regina explained how those two women encouraged her through the dark moments she experienced as a new resident in a new place and also as a new mom at 33—much later than most of her peers.

Regina told the group how she shared her uncertainties about living in suburbia, her questions about God and men, and her insecurities about being a mother. Hannah and Mary Ellen listened, smiled, and prayed. Regina learned to trust that these women weren't trapped in a role as her mother had been. These women were living deeply satisfying, happy lives. Regina wanted her life to be like theirs. She met with Hannah and Mary Ellen regularly over a two-year period. The most important impact they made on Regina's life was to teach her to trust that God loved her just as much as He loved any man and that, as a woman, she had a special, irreplaceable fit in the world.

Hiding from Myself

Regina's story is about a woman who came out of hiding. What happened immediately after Adam and Eve ate the forbidden fruit and their eyes were opened? They felt shame about their nakedness and sewed fig leaves to hide their bodies from each other. What was it that they hid? They hid their masculine and feminine differences. Just as the most immediate response to sin was threatened sexual identity, the most natural reaction to feeling threatened was to hide. Then they tried to hide from God—in the bushes, of all places. Hurting and hiding is often how God finds us today.

Adam and Eve's healing began that day in the garden when they came out of hiding and responded to the voice of God. God began the healing process by sending them out of the garden before they ate of the tree of life and existed in their sinful condition forever. Before He sent them out, He killed animals to provide skins to clothe them. This is a picture of how God heals us. The shed blood of the animals and the clothing crafted by God from their fur is a picture of Jesus Christ and His robes of righteousness that His shed blood enables us to wear. God's thoughtful and wise provision reveals how ineffective and empty the ways we try to cover our pain really are. Just as fig leaves would hardly protect Adam and Eve from the environment outside the garden, emotional cover-ups won't resolve the problem of threatened sexual identity.

We don't see many people walking around in fig leaves these days, but every day we do meet people who are hiding because of wounded sexuality.

All women (and men) are wounded. The wounds come in different ways at different times, but the pain is a reality known to all of us. Our automatic response to our woundedness is the same as Adam and Eve's—we try to find a way to cover up and protect ourselves against further damage. We desperately seek ways to keep ourselves from getting hurt again. As each of us tries to cover up, we use different strategies to accomplish this task.

How Do You Cover Up?

I invite you to take the following quiz to find out how you cover up. Place a check next to the statements with which you agree or to which you can answer "mostly true."

Type A

• Are you aware of major hurts in relationships, and have you forgiven your offenders?   _____

• Do you recognize the value you bring to church, family, and society because of your feminine perspective?   _____

• Can you recognize and identify male and female characteristics in yourself?   _____

- Do you experience God as both a just God and
  a nurturing God?   _____

Type B

- Do you feel trapped as a woman?   _____

- Would you say that being a woman has meant
  being taken advantage of in some way?   _____

- Do you feel unhappy about your relationships but
  helpless to do anything to change them?   _____

- Do you feel that your femininity has been damaged
  or stolen from you?   _____

Type C

- Do you feel that women have specific roles they
  should fulfill in church, home, and society?   _____

- Do you believe that if you follow certain rules
  carefully, your life should please God and He
  will bless you?   _____

- Do you try to change the ones you love?   _____

- Do you feel angry and bitter about how your life
  has turned out?   _____

Type D

- Do you find your greatest joy as a woman in how
  people respond to the way you look?   _____

- Do you spend most of your extra money on clothes
  and beauty products?   _____

- Do you struggle with your security as a woman when you don't look your best? _____

- Do you spend a lot of time thinking about how you look and how people respond to your appearance? _____

Type E

- Do you have little sympathy for people who can't seem to get their lives together? _____

- Do you believe that God helps those who help themselves? _____

- Do you have your life pretty much under control? _____

- Is it difficult for you to accept help from others? _____

Type F

- Do you feel that you constantly have to prove that women are just as good as men? _____

- Do you find it more difficult to trust men than women? _____

- Do you think you should be more connected in relationships but aren't sure how? _____

- Do you feel that you constantly have to defend yourself as a woman? _____

Type G

- Do you share your feelings only when you think others will agree with you? _____

- Could you say that you have no enemies?   _____

- Would most people describe you as kind, gracious, and good-natured?   _____

- Do you always try to do what others expect of you?   _____

Which type or types did you check most often? See the next section to discover what the different types are.

To Summarize

The types of women reflected in the foregoing quiz are not scientifically identified personalities. Rather, they are offered as a perspective on how various people respond as women in this world. Look again at your answers. No one woman responds exclusively to one category, but you probably tend to relate to the world as one type more than another. No one arrives at any of these types effortlessly. We are shaped by our life experiences, good and bad.

Type A—Contented Woman

Regina is a Type A woman. A few years ago, she would have been a Type F. Nearly all of us aspire to the contentment she enjoys. It makes her attractive to others in the deepest sense. She is a woman free to recognize her unique wounds of womanhood. She has discovered the medicinal power of forgiveness in healing those wounds. She has a healthy, balanced view of God as well, which enhances her value in the church and in society. She isn't perfect, but her deep relationship with God has transformed her pain and personality. In the freedom of His love, she has discovered her uniqueness and is eager to follow His direction for living in this world.

Type B—Victimized Woman

Quiet, retiring Judy has been damaged by forces she could not control. That did not keep those forces from identifying her as the culprit—from loading on the guilt. Victims almost always are given the impression that they are responsible for their woes. As an adult, Judy relates to others dysfunctionally because in her childhood it was the only kind of relationship she learned. She has no inkling of the dignity and value she possesses. She expects only to fall prey to the next abuser who enters her life.

Type C—Rule-Keeping Woman

Sharon, who tried to be the perfect wife, is a Type C. To her, rules are tools, not ends, and their misuse makes her angry and defensive about her place as a woman. Her long years of obeying the rules, however, appears to have been in vain. No wonder she is disillusioned and bitter.

Type D—Beauty-Obsessed Woman

Joy is a Type D woman. Unconsciously, she falls for every scheme of the advertising world. She is the first to try out the claims of every new anti-aging cream that hits the market. She has picked up the subtle message the world is constantly giving to women—that they are only as valuable as their sex appeal. Naively, many women believe that Christian women can't be seduced by such an unchristian agenda. Although we may dress more modestly, we don't differ in our desperate attempts to be beautiful. The more desperate we are for outward beauty, the more likely it is that we are using it as a way of concealing how ugly and worthless we feel inside.

Red-haired and energetic, Joy is a homemaker, volunteer, and part-time dress shop clerk. She has two daughters and a successful husband. She works only to keep herself and the girls in the latest fashions, which her husband avers is a waste of money. Joy looks and dresses like a much younger woman. When you see her, you think you are seeing a woman who is perfectly delighted with life. You don't notice right away that she is missing something crucially important, but she knows it. And it doesn't take others long to grow weary of her shallow conversation. Joy is definitely a Type D.

Type E—Controlling Woman

We all know this kind of woman. She has the world in her hands—or so it seems. She can make things happen. She can successfully organize the corporate world or the church social, but she does it all so beautifully that you don't always recognize how distant she is from real relationships. She knows everybody but is close to no one. She may look as if she's in control, but beneath her tough exterior she is crying out for intimacy with others.

Diane is usually the center of attention. She is the only one Regina invited who already knows a little about everyone present. If you need something, she becomes personally challenged to provide it. The problem is that her ex-husband didn't appreciate her distance. She has custody of her children but feels that they need something she can't give. She doesn't have a best friend; she just knows everybody. Can you understand how Diane fits the Type E—always in control, in good ways and bad?

Type F—Defensive Woman

This woman is deeply afraid of her own femininity. She usually feels she looks like a woman on the outside, but inside she tries to cover up her desperate fear that she is missing something. She fears men the most. Deep down, she is terrified that a vital relationship with a man would reveal that she really doesn't quite measure up. Sometimes she competes with men, thereby disguising how much they threaten her very existence.

Brenda is sitting on the patio next to Judy, whom she knows from the singles' group. Brenda is a successful businesswoman. She has her own house, dog, cat, car, and good girlfriends, but she just can't find Mr. Right. Her deepest desire, as far as she is aware, is to complete her hopes for "happily ever after" with a man and a couple of kids. She just can't figure out why she is always the bridesmaid and never the bride. Brenda fits Type F to a T.

Type G—People-Pleasing Woman

A people-pleasing woman is always trying to make other people happy. She would never raise her voice in public; that is unbecoming to a woman. She is kind, sweet, and lovely—and scared to death to let anybody really know her.

Faye's chair is scooted back behind the others. She is quiet but not withdrawn. She wears a constant smile throughout the meeting. She is married to a church leader, has three well-mannered children, and is first on everyone's list when there is a job to be done at church. Faye is a Type G woman, ever smiling, ever willing, never scandalous, yet always confused about why she isn't as happy on the inside as she looks on the outside.

Can you identify with one or more of these types? I've noticed that most women, including myself, relate to the world as Types B through G. We find a role that we are comfortable with that seems to help us manage the pain in our lives. Each of these roles or types works for us to a certain degree, but they are incomplete. They lead us to security of our own making, while God offers us security in a relationship with Him. He wants to draw us out and give us a vision of who we really are. He invites us to come out of hiding, to come into His presence, to find out how He made us and why we are here.

In the next chapter, we'll find out what our Healer wants for us as the women He created us to be.

CHAPTER TWO

What Does God Want for Women?

Ephesians 1:17–19 is a prayer Paul prayed for men and women he loved and cared for.

I ask—ask the God of our Master, Jesus Christ, the God of glory—to make you intelligent and discerning in knowing him personally, your eyes focused and clear, so that you can see exactly what it is he is calling you to do, grasp the immensity of this glorious way of life he has for Christians, oh, the utter extravagance of his work in us who trust him— endless energy, boundless strength! *(The Message)*

Why don't women clearly see what God is calling them to be? Perhaps we are confused about the answer to the question, What does God really want for a woman?

Sharon could answer that immediately. She had a whole list, and she had lived it out for 17 years. She tried to be the perfect Christian wife. She stayed home with her kids while they were young; then, after they started school, she got a job and surrendered her whole paycheck to her husband. She also let him make all the decisions in their family. But today she was one angry woman. She felt she had been slighted by God. She had done everything right, but He hadn't come through for her. He hadn't made her husband the man she wanted him to be.

Judy, on the other hand, had no idea what God really wanted; she was only sure of what she wanted. She wanted to stop hurting. She wanted out of the pain. She thought God would take away all of her pain when she was saved. Didn't the fact that she believed that God and Jesus were real and that Jesus' death had dissolved the sin separating her from God count for anything?

Brenda, Diane, Joy, Faye, and Regina could recite their own feelings about God and what they thought He wanted. How about you? What do you think God wants for you?

Time for You

What do you think God wants for your life?

_____ To be somber, not to wear makeup, and to serve others.

_____ To always be busy, doing things for the church, community, and family.

_____ To be a good citizen by being organized, involved, and dutiful.

_____ To spend time getting to know Him and discovering how to serve Him.

_____ Other

Along my journey toward getting to know God, I have discovered some of what He wants for me. I think He wants the same for you. He wants us to approach Him with confidence, and He wants us to know and experience Him as the Creator of our souls, who is able to show us who we really are. This is quite different from the roles presented to us by the church, the media, and feminists.

Many Christian women, like Sharon, try to define and live a religious role when it comes to femininity. They believe that if they focus on being hospitable, quiet, and meek and doing everything the Bible says a good Christian woman should do, then God will love them. But God doesn't want us to perform for Him. He doesn't want to give us a list of rules, with the promise that if we obey them perfectly, we will get everything we want. Rather, God wants us to get to know Him better because by doing so, we will take on more and more of Christ's characteristics.

Another group of women believe the media's view that women are valuable only if they are young and beautiful. Joy had succumbed to almost every message that advertisers offered women. She believed she was worthwhile only if she was beautiful. Sex appeal, white teeth, expensive perfume, designer clothes, and carefully applied makeup to her were indispensable because they told her that she was OK as a woman. But God wants us to be discerning about what the world offers us and tells us we need to be.

A third view of what a woman should be is offered by feminists, who believe that women not only can do anything men can do, but they can also do it better. A woman's value, feminists say, is in having a career and being independent. Again, God doesn't want us to embrace the rhetoric of a feminist society, as Regina did for a time and as Diane and Brenda were still doing. He wants to give us an anchor for our souls through relationship with Him. Most of all, He wants us to know that we belong—and not just *that* we belong, but *how* we belong.

God Wants Us to See How We Belong

Luke 10:38–42 records an episode of Jesus' earthly interactions with a couple of women. I just love this story because it is about an experience that all women can understand. It is simple, but it offers something to every woman.

As the story goes, Jesus was in the home of Martha, who had a sister, Mary. While Martha was busy with the many preparations involved in hosting such an important guest accompanied by so many followers and supporters, Mary was sitting at Jesus' feet, oblivious to the stresses the extra folks meant to Martha. Martha complained to Jesus, quite expecting Him to take her side and instruct Mary to get up and help her. Instead Jesus said, "Martha, Martha, you are so busy with so many things, but Mary has discovered what is best, what can never be taken from her" (Luke 10:41–42, paraphrase mine).

God says the same to me. "Debi, Debi, you're so busy with so many things. You worry whether people like you; you wonder how to make everyone happy. Find out what is best. Don't keep seeking from the world what only I can give you." Have you heard Him say that to you, too?

God offers each woman the same gift Mary received. He offers Himself, His time, His power, His wisdom. He invites us to sit at His feet and discover what happens to us when our souls reflect His image. Mary sat at Jesus' feet and found herself receiving what was really important and what could not be taken from her. She didn't care about gaining the approval of her sister or the men present by displaying her caretaking skills. Rather, she sat with Jesus and listened. Finally the core needs of her heart were being addressed. After years of searching, she had found healing ointment for her soul. The passion a man could give or the approval Martha could grant could not compare with this medicine. Once Mary had tasted this life-giving relationship, she knew what Martha did not—that the meal preparations could wait.

What held Mary captive was the image her soul was created to reflect. She saw Jesus and everything her life was meant to be. She heard His voice and knew He spoke the truth about who she was and what her purpose was in this world. She was no longer deceived by attempting to gain self-worth through earthly avenues. Her ears heard the story of her own life. She didn't move from her Lord's side because as He spoke, the mysteries plaguing her soul were solved. Suddenly, she knew why her life had been so meaningless. She had been created to reflect God's image, and anything other than that would leave her feeling empty.

Unbroken Image

Women constantly consult mirrors to make sure the images being reflected are suitable to present to the world. Hair perfectly coifed, makeup meticulously applied, clothes ironed and clean, shoes polished—now we are ready. We have created our image, the image of womanhood.

But this earthly image pales in comparison with the image God holds of us. We often don't recognize that each of us has special features of God Himself inside of us. We focus so much on how we look on the surface that we become oblivious to the most important image, the one that can't be taken away, the one that doesn't turn gray or wrinkle with age.

In Genesis 1:26–31, God shows us why we are valuable as women. We are His image-bearers. God created man and woman in His image. The distinctions between the sexes combine to create a reflection of the mysterious image of God. Why do women spend so much time looking into mirrors, yet miss this truth?

Judy rarely looked in mirrors, but when she did, all she saw was fat. She had lived with it for such a long time that she didn't want to change it. She just wished that other people would stop saying,

"You have such a pretty face." She might say she rejected her image in the mirror because of the fat. But if the truth were known, the fat was what kept her safe. It had been what had helped her survive womanhood. What she rejected about the image she saw in the mirror was the image itself. It could be fat, skinny, beautiful, or ugly; her hatred of herself kept her from recognizing the beautiful image of God that He Himself had made in her.

Sharon looked in the mirror, and all she saw were wrinkles. They didn't shock her as much as they did friends who hadn't seen her in a while. But she knew they were there. Her anger, which created those crevices in the first place, kept her from seeing the beautiful image that God saw.

Joy consulted the mirror a minimum of 20 times a day. If she liked what she saw, she had a confident, happy day. But more often she hated what she saw. Carefully applied outside beauty couldn't conceal the ugliness Joy felt in her heart and soul.

Diane and Brenda had nearly identical reactions to a glance in the mirror. They both saw women validated in a world of work and success but bankrupt in meaningful and satisfying relationships.

Then there was Faye. She rarely had time to look in mirrors because she was so devoted to the cares and concerns of her family and the people in the community. She didn't realize it, but she had made them a mirror. She looked in the direction of those she cared for, and if they had smiles on their faces, then Faye liked herself. However, if her husband, daughter, PTA officer, pastor, or anyone else wasn't happy with her, Faye felt ugly and rejected.

When Regina looked in the mirror, she saw a woman whose life had been changed by God; she saw a woman who no longer was driven by her insecurities to compete with other women. She felt blessed by who she was. She longed to serve and minister to others. Still, she had established strong boundaries around her time for herself and her family. Year by year, the reflection in the mirror, more and more, resembled the character of Christ. Regina didn't label the Bible as a tool of patriarchy as she once had. Now she saw it as the only hope for women everywhere. Her search had brought her to a point of embracing the image of God inside her and exploring how to more fully display who God was through the way she lived her life.

That Was Then, This Is Now

Genesis 1:26–31 describes how God met every need of the man and the woman and how they ruled the earth and animals. There was no need for the woman to think about being loved. She entered a world uniquely suited to give her love. That world was created by the very One who created her. Everything He made was for her to enjoy. She was created to enjoy the love of a man. She was created to cultivate the garden God provided for her. She was created to commune with the God of the universe in direct and transparent sanctity.

Unfortunately, this story didn't end happily. Sin scarred the world so drastically that now love and provisions must be salvaged from the wreckage. The wise woman will look beyond creation and man to find her truest sense of love. She will recognize that the love her heart was created to enjoy is found first through love from God. But the foolish woman will keep trying the earthly avenues. She will try to make her friends, husband, or children react to her in certain ways. Though she is desperate for love, her methods of obtaining it often drive people away.

Let's consult the only woman who knew firsthand what it is to live in the luxury of perfect love. Eve was the only woman to know a world that gave her everything her soul longed for. She also knew what it was to live the love-limited plight we experience. What can

Eve teach us about love and how to live with it and without it, while positively influencing our world?

The Hometown Hero

The events in Eve's life described in Genesis 1–3 are so radical that we sometimes forget God has more to tell us about her. As the early church writers explored and formulated doctrines, they professed strongly negative thoughts about Eve, based on those passages. Apparently, they didn't spend much time meditating on Genesis 4. When you read that chapter from Eve's perspective, her story emerges as a bittersweet one of faith, hope, and love in the midst of heartache.

In Genesis 4, the focus is on Cain and Abel and their sordid story of jealousy, murder, and sin. We tend to forget that Eve was right there through it all, living the horror. Imagine yourself in her place for a moment. You have two sons, one highly favored of God and another you love just as well, sulky though he may be. Now imagine what happens to a mother's heart when the dark one murders the bright one.

I worked at a certain place for a number of years. At first I was blessed with increasing financial benefits, but as the years passed, I found my benefits being dropped one by one. It didn't seem fair, and I became increasingly angry. I couldn't believe that I had faithfully put all those years of my life into a job for which I was reaping less and less.

I wonder if Eve felt anger like mine. Perhaps more? She lost so much more. Think of the major adjustments she had to make. Can you imagine being evicted from the Garden of Eden and thrown into a cold, cruel world? But if Eve was angry, it didn't last long. Her story is one of a woman who continually moved forward despite the painful realities the world dumped on her. Despite incredible defeats, it appears that Eve's trust and love relationship with God grew stronger.

We have only three verses that tell the rest of Eve's story—Genesis 4:1, 2, and 25—but they contain a powerful example for women to follow.

> *Verse 1:* Now the man had relations with his wife Eve, and she conceived and gave birth to Cain, and she said, "I have gotten a manchild with the help of the LORD."

> *Verse 2:* And again, she gave birth to his brother Abel. And Abel was a keeper of flocks, but Cain was a tiller of the ground.

> *Verse 25:* And Adam had relations with his wife again; and she gave birth to a son, and named him Seth, for she said, "God has appointed me another offspring in place of Abel; for Cain killed him."

These three verses, especially the quotes from Eve, guide me to the secret of living in a world without the love I was created to receive: Trust in God.

In verse 1, Eve praised God for His goodness to her when her first son, Cain, was born. She realized she didn't deserve anything. In spite of the pain of childbirth, she knew that God loved her deeply. She continually looked to God as her help and strength.

Eve may have been evicted from the garden, but she was blessed with two sons in spite of this. Then the worst ordeal of her life struck when the child for whom she praised God murdered her second child. What a blow! I probably would have felt like giving up at that point. I probably would have said, "Why go on? Why even try to make life work outside of the garden? Why trust God?"

But verse 25 reveals this wasn't at all Eve's attitude. Despite the pain, the defeat, the mess, she kept moving forward. She trusted God to sustain her throughout the years He gave her life on this planet. When she gave birth to a third son, she acknowledged God once again, perhaps in an even deeper way, as the One in whom she trusted.

Eve didn't demand love from her husband and children. She received the love they gave her, but she always relied on her true source of love: her relationship with God. He was the anchor for her soul as she lived in a troubled land.

How do we get to this place of peace where Eve seemed to be? How do we develop such a deep connection to the One who loves our souls that we gain a workable perspective on life and our problems? We begin by seeing how much God loves us. We discover this by looking at Him and not at our circumstances. When we discover God as our loving Creator, we discover what can't be taken from us. Like Mary sitting at His feet, we receive a healing balm for our souls.

Women Are Special

Women are unique and special to God. We each have an image beyond the one we see in the mirror. We don't just resemble Aunt Sally on Father's side. We resemble the Almighty! Can you look beyond the mirror to see that image? It is this image we must get to know. The image of God in us is our true beauty. We can chase all kinds of earthly dreams to find happiness, but these will never fulfill the longing in our souls to reflect and fulfill the image God placed in us.

Judy, Sharon, Joy, Diane, Brenda, Faye, and Regina each felt in a different way that their femininity had been stolen or compromised, and this blocked them from recognizing the image beyond the mirror.

Judy, the victimized woman, longed to see herself as valuable.

She just couldn't escape from that dirty, disgusting view she held of herself. The abusers in her life had robbed her of any desire to be a woman.

Sharon, the rule-keeping woman, had tried hard to be the epitome of a godly wife and mother, the quintessential feminine role. Now she was angry, and why not? God had tricked her by demanding the impossible and then failing to reward her efforts. He thereby stole her confidence in femininity.

Joy, the beauty-obsessed woman, lacked any real sense of value in femininity. Through her appearance, she actually overidentified as a woman. Her hair and nails were styled to perfection. She dressed like a model even when she was home all day. And yet she always felt put in her place, and it wasn't a very comfortable place. She had become programmed to believe that a woman should stay in the background until the men in her life wanted her. How could that possibly be enough to make life seem worthwhile and fulfilling?

Diane, the controlling woman, wondered if some portion of femininity was missing from her gene pool. According to the world, she had it all: kids, a great job, and even freedom from marriage. And yet she felt she was missing something. She didn't feel she was really woman enough.

Brenda, the defensive woman, was frightened of her femininity. She was denied a safe environment in which to be a woman. Even with her successes at work, she sensed that her colleagues, especially men, thought she had climbed the career ladder as quickly as she had because she was the token woman. That belief robbed her of her dignity.

Faye, the people-pleasing woman, the quiet, ever-smiling servant, was overwhelmed by the tasks of womanhood. She often found herself out of strength and out of ideas for keeping everyone satisfied. Her femininity per se was not at risk, but she was plagued by the feeling that this very femininity, with its demands for servant-hood (even martyrdom of a sort), was destroying her. Her life seemed to be galloping out of control.

There was a time Regina felt as guilty and bad about herself as the others. After she became a Christian, she was tortured by the reality of her abortions, and for a time, she thought her femininity could not be restored.

The truth is that our femininity *cannot* be stolen from us. We can mislay it for a time, or refuse it. We can use it to hide from our deep sense of insecurity. But no one can take the gift God breathed into us—His image.

Do you own one of Cindy Crawford's exercise tapes? Did you buy it because you really believed that you only have to do her workout three times a week and you will end up looking like her? We can always hope, I guess. But the truth is, even if we could all magically become beauty queens, our lives would not be healed. The image of God is not something we wear on the outside—it comes from within. It glows brighter as we come to a deeper and more nearly pure relationship with Him. It develops over time spent with Him. It is unleashed as we break the chain of lies we've believed about our image as women. When we finally see who we really are, we see how we fit in the world.

What kind of image do you see when you look in the mirror? Do you see a valuable, confident, capable woman? You can. I won't promise you Cindy Crawford abdominal muscles, but I can promise you the image of God. Why? Because it's already there. Even before you became a Christian, it was there. In the power of Christ and through the eyes of the Holy Spirit, you can begin to see your true image in that mirror. You can escape the bondage that prevents you from seeing who you are to God. Let me show you in God's Word what it means to be a woman. Open up your heart and your life to His healing of your femininity. Let's journey together until you can look in the mirror and see for yourself that there is nothing like a woman, and no other woman is quite as special as you.

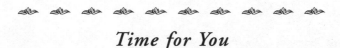

Time for You

What do you hear God saying to you through what you've read so far?

What image do you see when you look in the mirror?

CHAPTER THREE

Women's Impact on the World

Women do two-thirds of the world's work, grow at least 50 percent of the world's food, and still find time to produce every single one of the world's babies.[1] Imagine what this world would be like if there were no women. As a *Twilight Zone* episode, good plot. As reality, bad news.

How do you like being a woman? Most of the women I ask say they wouldn't have it any other way. We like that we are women. We don't like some of the injustices we face, we struggle with our relationships, and we often find ourselves vulnerable in a dangerous world. But, all in all, we would not change places with men for any reason at all.

What do you enjoy most about being a woman? Most women respond to this question by stating they like the depth and warmth, the connectedness, of their relationships. They like that they know what is going on in the lives of their spouses, children, friends, mothers, and others. By and large, women cocoon themselves in an intricately woven fabric of relationships.

Hollywood portrayed this virtue of womanhood poignantly in the movie *Steel Magnolias* as the principal character, Melyn, made notable observations about the differences between men and women when it comes to coping with death. The death in this case was that of her daughter, who succumbed in her twenties to complications from diabetes. Gathered at the young woman's bedside in the hospital were her husband, father, and mother. As the final seconds of her life were escaping, the men left the room, unable to watch her die. Nothing could have dragged Melyn away. At the funeral, Melyn commented on the men's behavior by musing that she thought men were supposed to be made of steel. She put a nice exclamation point on the privilege of being a woman with, "I realize as a woman how lucky I am. I was there when that wonderful creature drifted into my life, and I was there when she drifted out. It was the most precious moment of my life."

There was only one person who could say the same about Jesus. That person was also a woman: His mother, Mary. What a privilege it is to be a woman!

Celebrate Womanhood!

As women, we have a lot about which we can be proud. Our lives are full of strength and softness, love and sorrow, laughter and tears, quietness and boldness, hope and courage.

I have an answer to Professor 'enry 'iggins's plaintive question, "Why can't a woman be more like a man?" It's because God didn't make her that way, and He had divine reasons for doing so. God made men and women similar but distinct from each other.

In his book *Love for a Lifetime,* Dr. James Dobson wrote, "We are not alike." Here are some of the ways he noted that men and women are different.

1. Men and women differ in every cell of their bodies. This difference in the chromosome combinations is the basic cause of development into either maleness or femaleness.

2. Woman has greater constitutional vitality, perhaps because of this chromosome difference. Normally, in the United States, she outlives man by three or four years.

3. The sexes differ in their basal metabolism—that of woman being normally lower than that of man.

4. They differ in skeletal structure, woman having a shorter head, broader face, chin less protruding, shorter legs and longer trunk. Boys' teeth last longer than do those of girls.

5. Woman has a larger stomach, kidneys, liver and appendix, and smaller lungs.

6. In functions, woman has several very important ones totally lacking in man—menstruation, pregnancy, lactation. All of these influence behavior and feelings. The same gland behaves differently in the two sexes— thus woman's thyroid is larger and more active; it enlarges during pregnancy but also during menstruation; it makes her more prone to goiter, provides resistance to cold, and is associated with the smooth skin, relatively hairless body, and thin layer of subcutaneous fat, which are important elements in the concept of personal beauty. It also contributes to emotional instability—she laughs and cries more easily.

7. Woman's blood contains more water and 20 percent fewer red cells. Since these supply oxygen to the body cells, she tires more easily and is more prone to faint. When the working day in British factories, under wartime conditions, was increased from 10 to 12 hours, accidents involving women increased 150 percent; involving men, not at all.

8. In brute strength, men are 50 percent above women.

9. Woman's heart beats more rapidly (80, vs. 72 for men); blood pressure (10 points lower than man) varies from minute to minute; but she has much less tendency to high blood pressure—at least until after the menopause.

10. Her vital capacity or breathing power is lower.

11. She stands high temperature better than does man; metabolism slows down less.[2]

One area in which research has determined gender differences won't really come as a surprise to most women. It is the area of sensitivity—to physical sounds and smells as well as to feelings. (Remember, we're talking about *most,* not *all,* women and men. Some men are more sensitive in certain areas than many women.) Scientific research tells us that women hear better than men do.[3] The authors of *Brain Sex,* a book describing these differences between male and female brains, put it this way: "Women are simply better equipped to notice things to which men are comparatively blind and deaf."[4]

Two researchers from the University of Los Angeles, citing a study comparing improving Olympic records over the past centuries, predicted that women would outrun men by the middle of the twenty-first century.[5] This prediction was met with controversy, sending the sporting world into a frenzy to explain the data. But the facts reveal that women are making the most of their opportunity to excel in sports. Another study found that in 1971 only 294,000 girls participated in high school sports, while in 1992, two million were participating.

A study cited in the *Dallas Morning News* found that both men and women think that women are more ethical.[6] (Again, that caveat: *many* women versus *many* men.) Some researchers dispute this finding, arguing that women *appear* to be more ethical because they haven't made the kinds of corporate decisions that men do and that when they do, women will be as "unethical" as men. Whatever the truth is, both men and women consider women to be the more moral sex. This same study also reported that women are less likely to lie, steal, or cheat, are less violent, and are more willing to work than men.

Stereotypically, the female is nurturing, self-sacrificing, and peaceable. What does this really mean? Feminists argue that this stereotype has kept women in bondage for centuries, so they encourage women to abandon or even abrogate the nurturing roles.[7] Yet, in the 1990s, we have finally come to see that these qualities are important. These stereotypical characteristics are virtues, not vices. We recognize that the world needs a lot of nurturing, self-sacrifice, and peacemaking to create and maintain harmony.

Time for You

How would you define womanhood?

What three or four components of your life most aptly define womanhood?

How God Made Woman

Albert Einstein asked one question most of his life: "What is light made of?" In all of his accomplishments, he never found the complete answer to that question; yet he did discover amazing facts about the world God created. From Einstein's work, we now know about the nature of gravity, molecules and atoms, deep space and light particles, and many other phenomena. Still, the answer to "What is light made of?" remains a mystery.

Similarly, the differences between men and women will remain mysterious connections to the God who is too awesome to be explained. Still, we can discover some important realities about the way we influence our world by understanding the way we were created.

Genesis 1 describes the creation of Adam and Eve as a single, unique event. It states that man and woman were both created in God's image. They were both blessed and charged with ruling the creatures of the earth, as well as producing offspring. But that isn't where the story ends. Genesis 2 has some amazing and exciting information about creation. In this chapter, God takes a breath and says, "Hold on, world, there are some specifics I've got to let you in on. This stuff is just too good to keep to Myself. Are you ready to hear it?" Then He moves on with the rest of the story.

Genesis 2:1–3 tells us about the seventh day when the Creator of the universe took time for rest and enjoyment. It follows the short summaries of each day found in Genesis 1. But beginning in Genesis 2:4, there is a change of venue. God backs up to the sixth day and goes over everything again, only this time He adds more details.

Genesis 2:5 first states that shrubs and plants of the field had not yet been created. Now, why draw our attention to that? Could God be revealing to us the sacred love that motivated the creation of the universe? Could He be showing us that all the creating He did was for a purpose? Could He be saying, "I didn't create those unique plants on day three because they need cultivating. I made them on the sixth day because that was the special day that I created human beings. Men and women will enjoy these plants for food and nourishment and also because they need something to do. Because they were made in My image, they need to be creative just as I am"?

I see two important themes in the Bible's detailed account of the sixth day of creation (Genesis 2:4–25). The first is *love;* the second is *order.*

Love

The creation story is first and foremost a love story. As we review the details God shares with us in Genesis 2, consider this question: What kind of God takes such gentle care in creating a universe? In fact, in Isaiah 45:10 when God is warning the people against complaining to Him, the Maker, about what He created, He states, "Woe to him who says to his father, 'What have you begotten?' or to his mother, 'What have you brought to birth?'" (NIV). Would you risk telling parents that you think they have an ugly baby? Certainly not. Why? Because the bond between the parents and the baby is so strong that the parents could never see their child the way you do.

At times I think of what God did as similar to preparing a nursery for a newborn baby. I remember the excitement I felt and the details I organized as I created the teddy bear room for my first child, Rachel. Everything was done to provide a warm and safe environment for her to call home.

Saint Catherine of Sienna (1347–1380) wrote this about God's love for us:

> Why did you so dignify us? With unimaginable love you looked upon your creatures within your very self, and you fell in love with us. So it was love that made you create us and give us being just so that we might taste your supreme eternal good. Then I see how by our sin we lost the dignity you had given us. . . . So you gave us your only-begotten

Son, your Word. . . . We are your image, and now by making yourself one with us you have become our image, veiling your eternal divinity in the wretched cloud and dung heap of Adam. And why? For love! You, God, became human and we have been made divine! In the name of this unspeakable love, then, I beg you—I would force you even!—to have mercy on your creatures.[8]

Order

The other important theme in Genesis 2 is order. God had a plan; He had an order and a purpose in everything He set out to do in the acts of creation. As we look at the specific details that God laid out for us in Genesis 2, we find why the order in which God created is so important. God made sure everything was right for woman to enter the world.

Do you ever wish the man in your life was more responsive to you? Do you ever feel that you have to stand on your head to get him to notice something? Don't you just hate it when you get your hair cut or change something around the house and your male friend or husband says, "Oh, that's nice." God didn't want one of those "Oh, that's nice" responses to His creation. So He set the stage just right.

First things first—God created man. He took a handful of dust and from that He made a magnificent complication of arteries, veins, organs, muscles, and bones. Then, into this physical entity, He breathed life. He gave this wondrous perfect physique the ultimate endowment, His very breath. This handful of dust was transformed into a living soul.

Next, God created that ultimate homestead—the Garden of Eden. It was fashioned specifically with man's needs in mind. It was a self-contained paradise, more magical and splendorous than we could ever imagine. We still have a need for a home like this. Have you ever noticed how the most attractive homes are complemented with beautiful landscaping? Even if the plants and trees aren't natural to the terrain, people will go to extremes to cultivate gardens of wonder. There has never been a garden of wonder that can compare with the garden God made. Genesis 2:9–17 gives us some details about this paradise. Verse 9 says, "And out of the ground the LORD God caused to grow every tree that is pleasing to the sight and good for food; the tree of life also in the midst of the garden, and the tree of the knowledge of good and evil."

The garden was full of every tree that was pleasing to look at and good for food. God thought of everything. Have you ever had a meal at one of those out-of-the-way restaurants that have the greatest food but less-than-perfect ambience? It makes your food more appetizing if it is served in just the right atmosphere. Well, this garden had ambience. The food was pleasing to look at and delicious, too.

Genesis 2:10–14 describes the rivers that flowed through the garden. The purpose of the rivers was to water the plants. But these weren't simply practical rivers, providing needed irrigation for the garden's shrubs. And they weren't like the Mississippi either. Living in the South, I think of rivers as muddy, grimy entities—raging in freshet and dreary in drought. The rivers God describes were more magnificent than anything we have ever seen. One river surrounded the land of Havilah, where there was gold, aromatic resin, and onyx. Try to imagine this wonderful garden with its rivers, plants, and trees. What would it be like to live there?

Into this paradise, God put man. But He didn't just place him there. He gave him all the instructions he would need to complete the happily-ever-after picture. He told him to enjoy his life in the garden and to feel free to eat of any tree, except the tree of the knowledge of good and evil (Gen. 2:15–17). And Adam was happy.

The Reason for Woman

It would seem that God had finished for the day. But He had something else in mind. Let's take a look at what God says in Genesis 2:18. "Then the LORD God said, 'It is not good for the man to be alone; I will make him a helper suitable for him.'" Now, everyone knows that God knew all along that He was going to create a man *and* a woman. After all, He's God. Do you think He just turned off His sovereignty button for a moment when He made that statement?

No, God is trying to get our attention. He wants us to notice how uniquely and purposefully He detailed the creation of the man and the woman. When God says, "It is not good for the man to be alone," it draws our attention to an important matter. The only time that a part of God's creation wasn't good was when the man was created without the woman. In God's opinion, a perfect universe needed both the man and the woman. The first mention of a woman was as the solution to the man's loneliness.

OK, so what's next? When you come to the solution to your problem and you decide that you need to make a woman, you make a woman, right? It's not hard for God. All He has to do is pick up a handful of dust and make a woman. But notice what He does in Genesis 2:19–20.

What God did next was to bring the animals to the man to see what he would call them. Adam cheerfully agreed to do the job. In the process, he made an important discovery. For the first time, Adam felt a need that didn't have an immediate provision. Adam realized he needed to be able to relate to someone like himself. He had no helper (Gen. 2:20).

That was exactly what God wanted. The time was ripe to add the final touch to His work of creation—the pièce de résistance. It was time to create the woman. God caused Adam to sleep, took one of Adam's ribs, and from the rib He created the woman (Gen. 2:21–22). When God brought the woman to the man, He got the reaction He was after.

Adam awoke, took one look at Eve, and said, "She is part of me. She shares my flesh and my bone. She is woman" (Gen. 2:23, paraphrase mine).

Not a bad way to make an entrance, wouldn't you agree? Ever since, women have been making entrances, at weddings, coronations, and other festive occasions. But no entrance was more perfectly timed or more wonderfully orchestrated than this first one—which was how God intended it to be.

The facts of creation confirm the truth that creation would have been incomplete without woman.

Today's Woman

All of that was great for Eve, but what about today's woman? Some women may ask, "If God made me and planned a special way for me to relate in this world, then why is my life such a mess? All I've focused on doing most of my adult life is following God."

I like the way Ruth Senter answered this question in her book *Longing for Love:*

> In Eden, [woman] did not have to prove her worth; she simply knew her worth. [God] loved her, didn't He? In Eden, she didn't need to understand His love; she simply opened wide her arms to it. She was forever in His heart and mind. Hers was the simple joy of knowing she was loved.
>
> But today she is a long way from Eden as she zooms

down the expressway, glancing frantically from her watch
to her rearview mirror to the speed-limit signs that remind
her she is going faster than her limits.[9]

The same God who took so much care in creating woman and
giving her a place in the world has not stopped doing so for
women today. God desired to restore Judy to the foundation of her
femininity, a femininity that no abuser could take away. He longed
to give Sharon the answers she craved. He wanted to lead Joy,
Diane, Brenda, and Faye to a deep sense of belonging in relationship with Him. He hopes to hold each of us tightly in the reality
that the healing begun for us through Christ will be completed one
day. All of us need a healing of our femininity to discover God
more fully and understand uniquely our place in the world.

"How do we do that?" you ask. "Where do we go from here?"

God says that a good way to turn to Him is in our brokenness
(Ps. 51:17). He actually wants us to come to Him in spite of our
messes. He invites us to turn them over to Him. So why do we
keep hanging on to them, trying to clean them up ourselves? Part
Two will shed some light on this puzzling issue.

Obstacles to Achieving a Healthy Feminine Identity

CHAPTER FOUR

The Source of the Mess

So far we've looked at how we were created in order to
understand our deepest longings. In Genesis 2, we
recognize that our feminine origins are deeply connected
to our relationships because woman was created differently from man and in the context of relationship with
him. This is the essence of our femininity. Our deepest
longing as women is to be in harmonious, mutually
dependent relationships with humankind. This brings us to
our pain. Our deepest pain as women stems from our relationships when we wrongfully presume upon people to give
us what only God offers. Our efforts to deal with our pain
on our own is what creates the messes we face in our lives.
You could look at it this way.

> Deepest Longing (Relationship)
> + Deepest Pain (Hurt in Relationship)
> + Effort to Fix Pain (Control)
> ─────────────────────────────
> THE MESS (Problems in Our Lives)

Relationships Are Central

Tackling our messes—what a job! To illustrate how we might begin, let me tell you about the garbage in our yard. A couple of months ago, I glanced out the patio door and saw some trash strewed across our backyard.

Where did that come from? I wondered. *Did some kids dump garbage over our back fence?*

Perturbed, I picked it all up. The next week, the same thing happened: garbage everywhere. Was the garbage man having a muscle spasm right beside our house?

As I cleaned up this latest mess, I came across an envelope addressed to my neighbors—the neighbors beyond the fence. I didn't think they were *that* kind of people. So I put on my Sherlock Holmes hat and inspected the backyard thoroughly. I discovered that when our neighbors put their garbage out for pickup, they stacked it against the back side of our fence. All that luscious, aromatic, doggy-tantalizing stuff just beyond the pale intrigued our basset hound, Happy. The mutt was stuffing his muzzle through the fence far enough to rip holes in the trash bags and carefully drag out all the goodies he could snag, piece by piece, before the garbage man got there.

Simply tidying up each week was at best a stopgap and did nothing to actually solve the problem. In fact, it produced increasing frustration. To do anything effectively, I first had to find the source of my problem. And note that the problem was recurring but not constant. Six days a week, our yard stayed clean.

Judy, Sharon, Joy, Diane, Brenda, and Faye all experienced times when their image as women felt good—when their backyards were clean, so to speak. They each had moments, even seasons, when they didn't feel plagued by problems. Judy felt loved after she became a Christian when special people, like Regina, entered her life and embraced her as never before. Until recently, Sharon felt valued when she was involved in the church, because people looked to her for leadership. Joy felt on top of the world every time her husband took her out for a special evening or surprised her with a weekend trip. Whenever Diane experienced a tender moment tucking her children into bed, she felt better than the time she won her toughest case. Every time Brenda got a raise or Faye helped somebody, they felt worthy. Relationships, you see?

The acceptance and support these women received were nice, but they didn't erase the pain of past rejections or inoculate them from new ones. Relationships, even with a newborn child, never go smoothly. The complications of life and relationships can leave us bankrupt and lonely. All too often, we don't know what to do about it.

How do you feel about yourself right now? Do you like who you are? Are you basically content with life and happy to get up in the morning? If you answer yes, I bet you are content with most of your relationships. So many times we judge ourselves by the state of our relationships. If we feel good or in control or needed, then our problems seem few.

I can speak from my own experience. I find that my own relationships tug so deeply at my soul, I often view my image and value as a woman by the quality of my earthly loves. That's why I try to get people to like me. I don't want to feel rejected. If I'm loved, I feel lovable. If I'm treasured, I feel valuable. I believe that these feelings are common to women. But the glow from being loved and valued in our earthly relationships fades. Somehow there isn't enough there to sustain us and restore our souls.

As women, we must first recognize how much our relationships influence our view of ourselves and then find the sources of our negative images. Where is this garbage coming from? I wasn't able to keep my yard clean until I got to the source of the mess. I explained the situation to my neighbors, and they readily agreed to place their trash bags elsewhere. Likewise, we won't be able to address the garbage in our lives until we face it at its source.

Judy, Sharon, Joy, Diane, Brenda, Faye, and Regina all had lives that were a mess to one degree or another. Though Faye dealt with her mess as a Type G and Sharon as a Type C, the origin of their messes was the same. The motivating factor of Types B through G is that we are trying to make life work for us in our own strength. Although we might succeed for a while, the effort is never fully satisfying. Continuing to live as a Type B, C, D, E, F, or G is like cleaning up the garbage one week, only to discover the backyard covered with even more trash the next week. If we really want to deal effectively with our messes, we need to get to the source of our problems. The first step toward doing this is to study Genesis 1–3—the creation, the temptation, the fall, and the curses.

The Creation

In Genesis 1–2, we see our deepest longing for relationship. Genesis 2:24–25 shows us what God wants our relationships to be: "For this cause a man shall leave his father and his mother, and shall cleave to his wife; and they shall become one flesh. And the man and his wife were both naked and were not ashamed." The essence of a man and woman's relationship is mutual dependence and oneness.

Even Adam and Eve's nakedness went beyond the physical. They were naked spiritually and emotionally as well as physically. They were completely exposed to each other—body, mind, and soul—and completely accepting of each other. Their differences didn't divide them. Rather, their differences became the foundation for their oneness. The fact that we were created for oneness helps us understand what is really going on in our souls as we live outside the garden. It helps us see what is at the bottom of the messes we live in.

The Temptation and the Fall

By reviewing the account of the temptation and curses in Genesis 3, we gain a perspective on why we need to evaluate our relationships to sort out the messes in our lives.

Flaws Are Love Marks

Have you ever broken a piece of china? It was probably one of your favorites and may have even been valuable. It always happens that way. Loath to throw it away, you tried to glue it back together, but it just wasn't the same. Even if the seam didn't show, you knew it was there; you knew how it should be. Other people, casual observers, would not notice, but you knew. A flaw is a flaw. But sometimes flaws are love marks.

Before I married Brian, I made my one and only quilt. Totally handmade, it took hours and hours over a one-year period. Brian and I met just at the time I was putting the finishing touches on it, and he shared in my excitement when it was completed. The first time I ever used the quilt was on our bed.

We had been married less than a month when we were hanging some pictures in the bedroom of our little apartment. Brian laid the hammer down on the bed, and when he went to pick it up . . . well, you can guess. He tore a small triangular rip in my beautiful quilt. He felt awful. I tried to cover up my feelings, but something deep inside me grieved. My perfect, beautiful quilt was flawed. Holding back my tears, I got out a needle and thread and sewed it up.

Ironically, at this moment, I can't think of a time I've ever noticed the tear. I would have to carefully inspect the quilt to locate it. In a way, it is now a special love mark. It makes the quilt unique and testifies to the special love Brian and I share.

God's love is much more intimate than my love for my quilt, but you can see the similarities in the way God might have felt when His perfect creation became flawed. It was disappointing, but He didn't hesitate to fix it. He set a plan in motion. People often question the reason God allowed evil to continue in the world after the flaw (or sin) happened. Many struggle to understand how a loving God would tolerate the heavy burdens sin has caused in our lives.

I don't have time to go into that subject, although I think it is legitimate and important. (Two excellent books on the topic are Phillip Yancey's *Where Is God When It Hurts?* and James Dobson's *When God Doesn't Make Sense.*) I do want to ponder whether the flaw in God's creation became a love mark. Is it a way for us to realize God's love more completely? In His love, He refused to throw His damaged creation away. His love rules His holiness. His love found a way to repair the flaw.

What was the flaw? It happened in Genesis 3. It was much more drastic than a slight tear in a quilt. The flaw in God's creation was like taking a beautiful quilt and ripping it to shreds. The original material is still there, but the original form doesn't exist anymore. From the moment Adam and Eve ate the fruit in the garden, the first threads of God's perfect creation were torn apart.

I hate to think of my own reaction, had the tear in my quilt not been so small and repairable. I can get really frustrated when things I value are damaged. Not God. Surely we get a glimpse of His stubborn love, for He knew that the threads to sew up this flaw could only be manufactured by His own Son's body and blood. Still, He never hesitated to mend what He created.

Satan's Strategies

Satan used two strategies to turn Adam and Eve from God, to get them to destroy their perfect world and create the mess you and I now live in. First, he chose to divide and conquer. He spoke to the woman first, because engaging both of them would have been more difficult. Second, he caused them to doubt God's word and character.

Divide and Conquer

For centuries, the early church fathers maintained that the woman was at best inferior to the man and at worst a deceptive seductress because she persuaded the man to sin after Satan spoke to her. It is true that Satan did address the woman first, but the man's whereabouts are often not considered. For years, I imagined this story unfolding in such a way that Satan found Eve alone in the garden, entered into a theological debate, easily won, got her to sin, and enticed her to seduce Adam into sinning as well. But this is not exactly what happened.

Genesis 3:1–5 does not make it clear that Adam was by her side as Eve spoke to the serpent. However, verse 6 says unequivocally that Adam was with her *while* she ate the fruit. Essentially, he stood silently by and watched the woman sin. In the early 1900s, many, beginning with Elizabeth Cady Stanton, began to consider Adam's passivity. Because of Adam's lack of action during the temptation, Stanton labeled him a "passive docile brute."[1]

In 1 Timothy 2:14, Paul stated, "And it was not Adam who was deceived, but the woman being quite deceived, fell into transgression." It appears that Eve's motivation for disobedience to God was different from Adam's. This gives me the impression that Adam may have used Eve as a guinea pig. If he had cared more for her than for his own life, perhaps he would have said, "Wait! If we're going to eat this, let me eat first. If I die, don't eat it."

The difference between how Adam and Eve were tempted was that Satan spoke directly to Eve, distorting God's word, whereas Adam was tempted indirectly through watching Eve's actions. He ate after it appeared nothing had happened to Eve. They responded individually for different reasons to the temptation.

Though they acted individually when they sinned, they experienced the result of their sin—guilt and shame—together. The first blast of a sin-scarred reality (the one you and I know too well) was experienced in the context of their relationship when they tried to hide by covering their nakedness with leaves. Alienation, the opposite of oneness and unity, was the most immediate effect of sin.

What must it have been like to know only good and suddenly be bombarded with knowledge of evil? And think of the damage to Adam and Eve's relationship. They had been created to perfectly complement each other in an ideal relationship. Instantly, their nakedness brought discomfort, and they quickly sewed fig leaves to shield themselves from the eyes of the other.

That's the way Judy felt the first time her father molested her. One night he came into her room, smelling of alcohol. As he violated her, she lay frozen, staring at the ceiling. Something about the look in his eyes and the places he touched her didn't seem right, even to a six-year-old. But what was she to do? She was a child, and he was her father. She thought she was supposed to trust him, so she began to distrust herself. Like Adam and Eve, she lay there, dazed by the reality of evil, even though she couldn't quite define what was going on.

Adam and Eve's nakedness triggered fear and a need to hide. Whereas they had once enjoyed oneness of body, mind, and soul, they now ran for the safety of the bushes. Each wanted to be protected from the eyes of the other. It is critical to note how they hid themselves: They didn't cover their feet or their heads or their mouths. They covered their genitalia. They felt ashamed of their sexual differences. Sin brought on a sense of vulnerability in the area of sexual identity. Both now sensed that it was in the areas that they were different that they could be hurt. Perhaps the knowledge of evil made the woman fear she could be used sexually or even raped. The man may have feared that his body could be ridiculed or considered unsatisfying. Whatever went through their minds, their actions were the same—they ran for cover.

Men and women are still running for cover today. When we feel threatened, we try to find a way to protect our vulnerability.

Judy's way of running for cover was to live as a victim. She kept mental records of everything that had gone wrong in her life, and her attention was set on enduring the next heartbreak that would come her way. She hid by running away. That was why she left her family. If Judy thought she was cornered, she felt trapped and helpless, like a deer caught in a car's headlights. Unresisting, she ended up being a victim because she didn't believe she had any other options. At the bookstore where she worked, she overheard that a student who was hired after her and who was dating the manager, had received a raise. Judy found this unfair, but she would never have thought of discussing it with her supervisor.

Regina found it astounding to talk with Judy. Whenever their conversation involved the suffering of another person, Judy was quick to compare the situation to some way she had suffered. As a victim, she carefully tallied the disappointments in her life and found masochistic comfort in being assured that life would never work for her. Judy had no concept of the reality Paul proclaimed in Philippians 4:13: "I can do all things through Him who strengthens me." Deep in her soul, Judy had built up a wall of doubt about God's goodness.

Doubting God's Goodness

Adam and Eve had experienced God in an unique way. For a while, they had enjoyed a perfect relationship with Him, a relationship in which their soul hunger—their innate need to relate to someone greater than themselves—was fully satisfied. They saw how God made everything in their world to please them. And yet, at the point they chose to eat the fruit, they doubted God's goodness. They were questioning God's motives and character. Was He holding out on them, denying them something wonderful and godlike, as Satan suggested? They, like Satan before them, sinned because they wanted to be like God.

If you are a parent, you know what it's like to have a child question the goodness of your decisions. From a very young age, children communicate their belief that you're holding out on them. I remember my nine-month-old son, Benjamin, wanting popcorn. There is something about the smell of popcorn that attracts even an infant. (I myself can barely go to a movie theater without eating some of the greasy stuff, even if I've just come from dinner.) But I knew that although it smelled good and looked good, it would not be good for him to eat. Benjamin's cries and attempts to grab the bowl I was holding were evidence of his inborn doubt that I was doing what was best for him. (In case you are wondering, I stopped eating popcorn in front of him until he was old enough to share in the pleasure.)

As we age, our doubting only gets more sophisticated. My doubts about God's goodness are apparent every time I labor to protect myself or control my relationships. Adam and Eve introduced us to this life of doubting. As Larry Crabb said, we're born doubters. "Doubt of God's goodness creates the terror of aloneness in an unreliable world, which leads to rage against God for doing too little to protect us from suffering." [2]

Do you ever find yourself reacting as Adam and Eve did? You probably never encountered Satan as a beautiful serpent, but every day he seeks to mislead you. His plan is to hook you by the pain you feel about your relationships and direct you to futile ways to gain control over this pain.

For instance, Judy felt so overwhelmed by the pain of having been sexually violated and her disappointment in the church's inability to solve her problems that every time she made a decision to move forward and something bad happened, she felt as if she weren't making any progress at all. Satan wanted her to feel hopeless and to focus on ending the pain by ending her life.

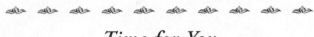

Time for You

In what ways does Satan tempt you to distrust God's goodness?

How do you feel threatened as a woman and try to cover up?

After the Fall

Life after the fall took a traumatic turn for Adam and Eve. Each of us knows the consequences of sin that began at the moment they both ate the fruit. None of us has been spared from feeling loneliness, the pressure to provide food and shelter, physical pain and illness, disappointments and heartaches. God also suffered the moment Adam and Eve sinned. Though His heart was broken, He didn't leave them to wallow in the consequences of sin. That day in the garden, He appeared to Adam and Eve and spoke words of hope and healing.

These words of hope and healing are commonly thought of as the curses. But when you understand the context in which God spoke them, you'll see the deep love and concern behind them. These words spoken centuries ago are no less important to us today as we struggle to live in a world marred by sin. In the next chapter, we will unlock the mystery of the curses and discover how they brought hope and healing to Adam and Eve, as well as how they can bring hope and healing to us today.

CHAPTER FIVE

The Curses: God's Healing Words

Why are recipes for conventional ovens different from those for microwave ovens? Even though you can cook many of the same foods in both types of ovens, you can't do it the same way because the appliances cook foods differently. You could look at the directions God gives to men and women in the curses in a similar way. Like conventional and microwave ovens, male and female human beings are different by design. Who would understand these differences better than God, who created them? That's why we should give considerable attention to the manner in which He speaks to men and women. There are important directions here that make living more palatable.

Both the man and the woman sinned, both hid from each other and from God, and both blamed someone else for their sinning. (Eve blamed the serpent; Adam blamed Eve and God.) But when God talked to them, He addressed them separately. What is the unique and specific information about life outside the garden given to us by the God who designed us? His words to the woman are found in Genesis 3:16. The man is addressed in Genesis 3:17–19. These passages are commonly referred to as the curses.

Before reviewing God's instructions, let's consider the mood in the garden. Here are a man and a woman who just moments ago enjoyed everything their souls longed for. But now their paradise is beginning to unravel, and they are on the verge of discovering the biggest mess they could ever imagine.

The Curses Describe Our Most Painful Realities

Have you ever made an impulsive decision that you regretted for years? I've counseled many people who have suffered enormous consequences for split-second decisions. Sometimes a momentary act can lead to a lifetime of suffering and pain. On April 19, 1995, a homemade bomb exploded in Oklahoma City. Thousands of people were affected by this tragedy. Whether they lived or died often hinged on commonplace decisions they made; for example, one person woke up sick and another went to work late. That day insignificant decisions and actions made the difference between life and death.

Adam and Eve made a simple decision that had catastrophic results. Their decision was a moral choice not to trust God. Although the pain of guilt was quick to strike Adam and Eve, the full reality of living in a sinful world revealed itself slowly. First there was the desire to hide from each other. Then they had to face their sin before God. Next they were kicked out of the garden, thereupon losing the many blessings they had enjoyed when they trusted God. Probably the most painful result of their sin was the moment they discovered that their own son Cain had murdered his brother. What greater anguish is there for a parent?

What is the purpose of the curses? Obviously, they don't represent even the tip of the iceberg of horror that sin set in motion. God didn't take the time to give a detailed account of the hideous influence evil would have on His wonderful creation. He didn't describe famines, earthquakes, wars, or pestilence. Rather, in pronouncing the curses, He addressed three essential realities, realities that I see as special love marks. The curses reveal how relationships between men and women will be disrupted by sin and how men and women will experience the pain of sin uniquely. The curses were not some kind of hocus-pocus intended to make life difficult for Adam and Eve. The curses were more like warnings about what life would be like from then on. They weren't extra punishments God threw in to drive His point home. They were instructions for life outside the garden.

In Genesis 3:9, God stepped in to deal with the mess the man and woman had created. He didn't jump down and deliver His just blow the minute they sinned. He didn't react the way I sometimes do when I discover one of my son's infamous messes (such as a watercolor painting that has turned into a huge black smudge all over the kitchen table) and say to him, "Benjamin, why did you do this? What were you thinking?" No, God came as He always had, in the cool of the day. Only He found a different response to His holy presence. Instead of finding two creatures eager to fellowship with Him, God found the garden deserted.

I can't picture this scene without smiling. I mean, can you imagine playing hide-and-seek with God? It reminds me of the times I played hide-and-seek with my daughter, Rachel, when she was four. She loved the game and wanted to play it again and again. The thing was, she always hid in the same place—behind the recliner. The hiding place itself didn't even conceal her whereabouts. I would count to 20 and then try to walk by without seeing her. I would go around the house looking in closets and under beds, pretending not to notice that she was right under my nose.

God, being a loving and respectful parent, pretended not to notice the man and woman hiding like cowards in the bushes. He simply called Adam's name and waited for the two to reveal themselves.

When the man and woman finally emerged, God continued to treat them with respect, asking Adam who told him he was naked and if he'd eaten from the tree God had commanded them not to eat from (Gen. 3:11). Again, God's mercy and patience are evident. It's like catching your child with his hand in the cookie jar and allowing him to admit the guilt, rather than jumping ahead to a punishment. Well, Adam knew he was caught, but instead of repenting, he blamed Eve and God Himself. Adam said, "The woman you gave me caused me to do it" (Gen. 3:12, paraphrase mine). Eve likewise fudged before a holy God and blamed the serpent for her own wrongdoing (Gen. 3:13). What a perfectly human scene!

God's responses to the three transgressors were unique and specific. To Satan, He laid it on the line (Gen. 3:14–15). The serpent went from the craftiest of created beings to the most humble and hated of beasts. Triumphantly, God let Satan know where he was headed. From the woman will come a seed (the first mention of Christ): "He will bruise you on the head, and you shall bruise him on the heel" (Gen. 3:15b). God's pronouncement on the serpent went right to the point: "I'll take care of you now, and I'll finish with you later by the seed of the woman you deceived."

The Distinctiveness of Pain Between Man and Woman

History has confirmed the truth of the curses: Men and women perceive reality differently. Women are more relationally oriented and men are more achievement oriented. This is why God addressed the man and the woman separately, even though they were affected by each other's curses. The life of toil ending in death directed to the man (Gen. 3:19) applied to the woman as well. Otherwise, women would not die. The curses describe the painful realities men and women would face as fallen persons.

In Genesis 3:17–19, God said to Adam, "'Because you have listened to the voice of your wife, and have eaten from the tree about which I commanded you, saying, "You shall not eat from it"; cursed is the ground because of you; in toil you shall eat of it all the days of your life. Both thorns and thistles it shall grow for you; and you shall eat the plants of the field; by the sweat of your face you shall eat bread, till you return to the ground, because from it you were taken; for you are dust, and to dust you shall return.'" The most painful realities for the man were in the area of his adequacy— his limited ability to evoke from the ground what he needed for life. He would confront constant obstacles as he labored to meet the needs of himself and others. The result was a sense of inadequacy.

In Genesis 3:16, God said to Eve, "'I will greatly multiply your pain in childbirth, in pain you shall bring forth children; yet your desire shall be for your husband, and he shall rule over you.'" The woman was cursed in the area of her relationships. The change in the relationship with her man and the realities of the differences in their body types and reproductive abilities would leave her in a position to experience discord rather than instant love. A woman's relationship pain would surface in a fallen world since men are stronger, do not carry the burden of reproduction, and are driven to achievement more than relationship. Her pain would stem from the fact that her relationships would not be what her soul longed for them to be. It was the law of sin, which entered their lives, that caused the problems of inadequacy (man's curse/greatest pain) and relationship disunity (woman's curse/greatest pain).

Do you now understand the source of your pain? Do you see how God made you for relationship? Knowing this doesn't diminish the trauma of your pain or provide a magic cure. It does give you a connection to God. It helps you see that He knows the messes in your life. These messes can drive you to God or away from Him.

Our Souls Are Not Made of Teflon

When we understand that our core relationships are central to our existence as women, we begin to understand how the image of God in us gets blurred by our human rejections. Our souls are not made of Teflon. Rejection sticks. It sticks firmly and tightly. It makes a baked-on gooey mess. Rejection blurs our vision of who we are. We begin to believe we are rejectable and therefore have a poor image of ourselves. This is far from the image God created in us and the image that Eve enjoyed.

I think of Patty, whom I met at a park while watching my children play. The initial image she presented led me to wonder whether she was mentally disabled. She wore a stained and wrinkled cotton blouse and the hem of her skirt was hanging down in places. Even her socks were rumpled. Her head was tilted forward, and she kept her eyes downcast, as if she were desperately afraid someone might notice her. As we spoke, she barely looked at me.

At first she seemed disconnected, not only from her image as a woman, but also from society. As our conversation developed, she began telling me some of her life story, a horror tale of hurt and rejection. She grew up in and out of foster care because of her mother's alcoholism. She hadn't seen her father since she was three years old and didn't know if he was dead or alive. She married an alcoholic, who had just divorced her, leaving her to raise their son alone. Disabled by depression, she was living on welfare. Throughout her life, she had been marred by cruelty and neglect. Patty's unkempt appearance reflected her despair.

I meet Pattys every day, women with compelling histories of pain and rejection, which they carry into every new relationship. They even carry them into their relationship with God. Most don't look like Patty on the outside, but digging a little deeper, I discover the same despair within. It's because our souls aren't made of Teflon. The rejection we all face because we live in a fallen world sticks fiercely to us.

What do we do when we're faced with a baked-on, sticky mess in the kitchen? Our only options are to throw the pan away (something Judy tried to do through her suicide attempt) or keep soaking and scrubbing it until we get the mess off. This kind of cleaning doesn't take away all the stains, however. The pan will never look as good as new. But it is usable and perfectly capable of fulfilling the purpose for which it was created.

I'm glad we have Teflon to make cleaning pans easier. I'm also glad that God will help us scrub away the baked-on scum that renders us unable to serve His purposes for us. I'm even more grateful that our souls aren't made of material that retains stains the way pans do. God has the power to heal our damaged souls so completely that they end up whiter than snow (Ps. 51:7).

The story of our pain doesn't end here. This longing for relationship isn't dangled before us like a carrot on a string. God doesn't show us how we were created so that we can feel trapped and helpless. Genesis 1–2 is the promise. We were conceived in love by a God who cares deeply for us. Our painful lives on earth with the effects of sin and rejection are the problem. The provision is in relationship with God through Jesus Christ.

Before we learn how to receive this provision, however, let's more fully and personally explore the problem in our souls—how to break free from our state of sin and rejection. We'll also discover how God responds to our sin and how He provides for our relationship needs in a fallen world.

CHAPTER SIX

*W*omen, Love, and Relationships

Judy, Sharon, Joy, Diane, Brenda, Faye, and Regina, seven women, represent thousands of relationships. When that small group got together, their interactions, feelings, and frustrations were not limited to the moment or to the people present in the room. Repercussions of each woman's complex web of relationships reverberated to the other women, each feeling the tugs in unique ways.

For instance, Diane, the controlling woman, was late for their support meeting one night. When she walked in, the dark cloud of anger that had accompanied her all afternoon swept in with her. She was not angry at any person in the room. The cloud had been generated by her conflict with a defense lawyer in a judge's chambers. Still, the palpable anger from that business encounter brought the conflict into the women's group. Diane's problem became Faye's problem, because Faye felt she could no longer discuss her sadness about her dog's injury when Diane was obviously so upset. Judy was resentful that

71

Diane had burst in so late and snatched the attention away from Faye. Sharon was glad for the distraction because she viewed Faye's problems as trivial. Brenda was hoping to get a chance to tell the others what an awful thing her father had said to her brother last week, but Diane's smoldering fury seemed to steal the spotlight. And Joy, the beauty-obsessed woman, who didn't always think deeply, was watching Regina to figure out the right way to feel.

We were created for relationships, but our relationships create problems in our lives.

What Are Women's Problems?

If we boiled down every problem of every woman who ever sat across from me in the counseling office, we would find one common bond: Women's problems are centered in their relationships as they seek to control the hurt they experience from them. As women struggle to understand their female identity, they need to realize the impact their relationships and their attempts to control them have on how they see themselves.

Your problem may be that you have a friend who is driving you nuts. She is always bragging to you about her children and puts your children down in subtle ways. Perhaps the problem is with your boyfriend—he won't commit, but you know he's the one for you. It could be with your ex-husband—he controls and uses you when it comes to the kids. It could be your fantasy life—you keep thinking that if you were married to someone else, you wouldn't be in so much pain. If we were in a room together and could each voice our biggest problems, they would be varied, but the bottom line would be the same. They would all be anchored in relationships.

Time for You

What is the biggest problem you are facing right now?
Does it involve a relationship?

Faye, the people-pleasing woman, disagreed with the suggestion that women's biggest problems are centered in relationships.

"My worst problem is that my phone won't stop ringing. That doesn't have anything to do with relationship."

"Isn't the phone a communication device? And doesn't communication mean relationship?" someone asked.

"No, not really," Faye said. "Most of the calls aren't personal. Most are salespeople and donation requests. Some are computers, not even a human voice! Oh, come on, girls! Don't you get scads of these telemarketer calls where the person mangles your name and reads off a pitch for a time-share offer? Or for magazines or credit cards?"

"Sure. You tell them to get lost. Why are those calls such a problem for you?"

Faye had to think about that for a moment. "I guess because I'm just too polite to say no. I always at least end up listening to the sales speech."

"That, my dear, is a problem based in relationship, even though it's a momentary relationship with strangers."

Even though relationships are central to women's problems, many women are often oblivious to the fact that their own behaviors are damaging to these relationships. In my professional practice and in the everyday world, I see women compulsively adhering to a cycle of damaging relationships that most don't even recognize as such.

The Cycle of Damaging Relationships

What exactly is the cycle of damaging relationships? It involves a need for love that leads to control over relationships.

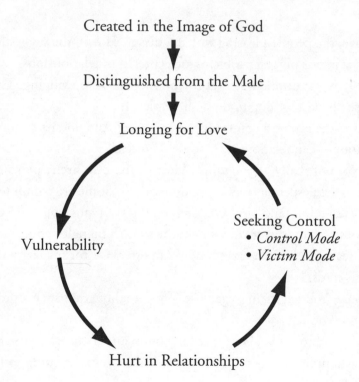

Created in the Image of God

Distinguished from the Male

Longing for Love

Vulnerability

Seeking Control
• *Control Mode*
• *Victim Mode*

Hurt in Relationships

Created in the Image of God; Distinguished from the Male

Brenda, like other women, was a female version of God's image in human beings. You don't have to be a Christian to be created in God's image. All men and women bear our Maker's mark. Max Lucado described this reality in his book *A Gentle Thunder:*

Why does a mother love her newborn? Because the baby is hers? Even more. Because the baby is her. Her blood. Her flesh. Her sinew and spine. Her hope. Her legacy. It bothers her not that the baby gives nothing. She knows a newborn is helpless, weak. She knows babies don't ask to come into this world.

And God knows we didn't either.

We are his idea. We are his. His face. His eyes. His hands. His touch. We are him. Look deeply into the face of every human being on earth, and you will see his likeness. Though some appear to be distant relatives, they are not. God has no cousins, only children.[1]

Brenda was different from men, and she recognized this. However, she refused to be thought of as "not as good as a man."

Longing for Love

Brenda was born into this world with a longing for love. This is a reality that Brenda had no control over. It was just a part of being human and part of the image of God in her.

I have had the privilege of giving birth to two children. They both came into the world hungry, cold, and pretty much out of sorts. My job was to nourish them and keep them safe and warm. They reminded me of little birds when they cried for food. With their mouths wide open, all they cared about was finding something to suck on that would satisfy the hunger in their stomachs. They would also cry if they were cold or too warm or if their diapers needed attention. Sometimes they cried because they just wanted to be held. They simply wanted someone to touch them and be close to them.

You've probably heard about the research showing that babies in hospitals who were held frequently thrived, while those whose basic needs were met but who weren't held did not grow as quickly, and some even died. There is no mistaking that we come into this world, not only with a physical hunger in our stomachs, but also with an emotional hunger in our souls for intimacy and love.

Brenda, being raised by imperfect parents, learned early in life that her love needs would not be met perfectly. Both of her parents worked, and although there was some connection with her mother, she often found her father to be a distant mystery. She could relate to Erma Bombeck's statement that when she was "a little kid, a father was like the light in the refrigerator. Every house had one, but no one really knew what either of them did once the door was shut." [2]

Vulnerability

Brenda depended on her parents and the other adults in her world for her love needs. She was also, of course, dependent upon them financially and biologically—that is, she needed them to provide food, clothing, and shelter. Human beings are dependent and vulnerable for a much longer period than animals. When my daughter was six, she sometimes acted as if she were six going on 16. There were days when she wished her parents would just go away and leave her alone. Although she was a bright little girl, if we ever had gone away and left her alone, she would not have survived for long. Sooner or later, the electricity would have been turned off, and the food in the cupboards would have been eaten. She was not old enough to take care of herself, however adult she believed herself to be.

We have been taught that being vulnerable is a bad thing, which is untrue. We each need to learn the strength of our vulnerability. The reason being vulnerable seems so bad is that most of us have tasted vulnerability only in the context of painful relationships. By experiencing our unique vulnerability in relationship with God, our view of it will be redefined. We will see that the place to get off this cycle of damaging relationships is actually at the point of vulnerability. In fact, we ought to use another definition of *vulnerable* that is more appropriate to a relationship with God. That definition is "openness." *Vulnerable* means "being hurt-able," but it also means "being open to" something.

Suffice it to say that, as far as Brenda was concerned, she was dependent upon her parents to meet her financial, physical, and emotional needs and thereby was vulnerable to neglect and hurt. Children have little control over how their parents meet their needs.

Hurt in Relationships

I asked Brenda to tell her most painful memory from childhood. She related this story:

> I didn't get much time alone with my mom, just the two of us. But this one Saturday afternoon, we went downtown to run some errands and shop a little. I was about eight. In a store window, I saw the most beautiful dress in the whole world. It was for dressy occasions, and I really didn't have anywhere to wear it. Our family rarely went to church or to dress-up events. But I just couldn't stop talking about that dress.
>
> Near the end of the afternoon, Mom took me back to this store and bought me not only the dress, but shoes and socks, a purse, and even a new slip. I was in heaven! When we got home, I just had to try it all on and model it for Dad, of course. I came prancing out, glowing—sashaying like a model. I was expecting a big smile on my father's face, but he looked furious. I was stunned.

He said, "You have no use for something like that. Take it back! All of it! And when you take it off, be careful with it." He returned it that very afternoon and pocketed the money.

I cried so hard and so long that I made a vow that I would never cry again. And I decided that I would never want anything that I couldn't get myself.

After all these years, Brenda still looked hurt. "You know, I don't think I ever got over it."

I don't think she did either.

All of us have experienced hurt in our relationships, beginning with our primary caregivers and continuing to this very moment. That's vulnerability. We all react to this pain in the same way. We want to stop it as quickly as possible, to block it off. Over the years, in order to minimize the amount of hurt people can inflict on us, we've all learned to be controllers to varying degrees.

Seeking Control

You may disagree with me at this point. Perhaps you know some very controlling women, but you don't consider yourself controlling and so you can't relate to this part of the cycle. Actually, there are two types of controlling women: overt controllers such as Brenda, and subtle controllers, or victims.

I quote Proverbs 14:1 quite often to women in marriage counseling. But the scripture doesn't apply only to married women. All women are described in this verse. "The wise woman builds her house, but the foolish [woman] tears it down with her own hands." I like this verse because it shows so realistically what women do. Both the wise woman and the foolish woman want love, and both of them use their own hands to get it. But the foolish woman ends up tearing down her own home by constantly nagging her husband or by trying to be her daughter's best friend when her daughter really needs a mother. The wise woman, on the other hand, builds up her home by having a strong relationship with God that allows her to encourage her husband even when he fails her and to provide guidance to her children and friends. The foolish behavior is motivated by a woman's drive to control love in relationships.

As mentioned earlier, there are two roles women fall into in their attempts to get love and minimize hurt: controller and victim. Both modes can damage or destroy relationships.

Control Mode

The controller tears down her home and any hope for relationship by keeping others at a distance through her demanding and obsessive nature. We all know this kind of woman. She is the nosy neighbor on sitcoms who is constantly telling other people how to run their lives. She is often married to a henpecked husband. She usually has some endearing qualities that keep people in relationship with her, but they are always kept at arm's length. Most often, people learn that they must walk on eggshells around her.

The desperate desire to control relationships brought painful and mysterious struggles into Brenda's life. She was a successful businesswoman in a large firm. She wanted to marry, but she just couldn't see herself with a man. Oh, she had dated quite a bit, but the men she didn't frighten away were never good enough. One of her worst problems was that at 39 she had finally discovered that she herself didn't know what "good enough" was.

As we explored this issue in her counseling sessions, she saw that no man would ever be suitable because she had decided when she was eight years old that she would never want anything she couldn't be sure she could get—and keep—herself. She could never be sure she could control a man enough to avoid being hurt. She was too afraid of making herself vulnerable to a husband the way she had been forced as a child to be vulnerable to her father. Instead, she sought control over her job, her house, her body, and her pets. Her controlling ways were damaging her relationships.

Victim Mode

The victim tears down her home and her life by ignoring her God-given instincts that people are using or hurting her and by allowing others to take advantage of her. She thinks she is being loving because she is always turning the other cheek. In fact, she is extremely self-protective. Her dependent passivity keeps people from knowing her and controls the degree to which they can reject who she is.

Faye's drive for control was masked by her sweet smile. You wouldn't think of her as a controller. You would say that she was being controlled by others, and on the surface, it certainly looked that way. But every time she said yes to another committee or made cookies for another event, she was controlling (or attempting to control) how people viewed her. In essence, she was buying others' approval with deeds. She hungered to be seen and liked. Therefore, she hid the parts of herself that she feared others would not like and made certain to display (to excess) the qualities she thought would impress them.

Judy, too, used the victim mode. She believed she was powerless to keep people from using her, so she almost invited them to do so. She maintained control by offering herself up as the victim, even unconsciously taking the first step. Subconsciously, she rationalized that she didn't have the power to make her life any different. She lived by a learned helplessness—believing she was unable to prevent others from hurting her.

Continuum of Control Modes

Here is a continuum of the seven personality types and how they control their relationships. A balanced personality would be in the middle.

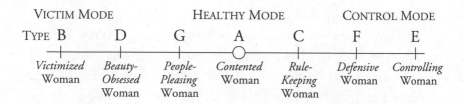

VICTIM MODE		HEALTHY MODE		CONTROL MODE		
TYPE B	D	G	A	C	F	E
Victimized Woman	Beauty-Obsessed Woman	People-Pleasing Woman	Contented Woman	Rule-Keeping Woman	Defensive Woman	Controlling Woman

To better understand yourself as a woman, it's important to understand how you tick, and that means seeing two things: (1) You need to recognize, acknowledge, and release to God your innate hunger for love, and (2) you need to recognize, acknowledge, and release to God this tendency of every woman to control relationships. We women cling relentlessly to a subconscious belief that if we can only attain control in our relationships, we will get the love we are after. We become so committed to this subconscious belief that in our drive to obtain love, we often appear to be driving away those who are closest to us.

Women's Unique Pain

What is the end result of handling problems and the drivenness for love and relationship through control? Unhappiness and misery. But there is some degree of relief through the effect of control. If there were absolutely nothing gained, women would have given up on control long ago. One of the trade-offs of control is safety.

Brenda felt a strong sense of safety in her black-and-white world where no one could hurt her because she didn't let anyone get close enough. Of course, at the same time she was also profoundly lonely—the downside.

Sharon, the perfect wife, took refuge in her set of ironclad rules. Shoehorning the world into a manageable set of parameters made her feel safe and comfortable. She believed, in fact, that she had discovered a way to control God (more technically speaking, her concept of God) and manipulate Him into making life work out for her.

King Solomon told us: "There is a way which seems right to a man [and a woman], but its end is the way of death" (Prov. 14:12). When we find ourselves experiencing pain in our relationships and try to manage it by controlling these relationships, at first it feels natural and right. It takes time to realize that we aren't getting the response we wanted and that the way that seems logical and right is really a dead end.

For instance, Joy tried to control her husband by being pretty and alluring, and she succeeded frequently enough to have made her control measures a habit. When he rewarded her efforts with a trip or money or jewelry, she felt great. However, she hated him and ultimately herself when the system failed and she couldn't get him to show her the attention and affection she wanted. But this was the only way she knew to make her fear of rejection go away.

As crazy as it seems, Diane, the pushy, get-things-done woman, controlled her fear of being rejected by rejecting others first. She automatically distrusted and tore down every effort her husband, Tim, made to love her. That robbed both of them of happiness. To make matters worse, she now had two kids who looked to her for a love she couldn't give because it was locked up too deeply inside of her.

Regina, the one who had come to terms with herself and with God, seemed to have it all worked out. Not quite. She struggled with her own control needs at times, but she had learned what to do with them so that she built her house up instead of tearing it down. She handled control needs by confessing her negative emotions to God. When she did, she found that He replaced her control efforts with love. True love respects the reality that people have free will. Regina realized that you can't change that fact and that ultimately no control ploy works well.

One of the ways in which Regina made a positive impact on women was by truly loving them. In love she desired their best and gently directed them to a relationship with God. However, she avoided taking responsibility for their responses. Spiritually and emotionally, she could point the way, but she had learned she couldn't drag a woman or man anywhere that person did not want to go.

This precept was nowhere more difficult to maintain than in her relationship with her husband. She prayerfully acknowledged her desire to be loved by him and accepted his limited endeavors at expressing his love. She did as Oswald Chambers suggested: "Drink deep and full of the love of God and you will not demand the impossible from earth's loves, and the love of wife and child, of husband and friend, will grow holier and healthier and simpler and grander." [3]

It's not that a woman's deep need for love differs from a man's. Rather, it is the degree to which she will go, and the sacrifices she will make, to create a sense that she is loved that distinguishes her experiences from that of a man.

Deep inside the female soul is a vacuum driven by a need for love in relationship. As a man shapes his identity and dignity around what he can accomplish, a woman's identity and dignity are determined by how successful she is in relationships. In large part, when a woman feels loved, look out, because she'll change the world for the better.

It is our woman's image that reflects the relational and creative aspects of God most fully. We are the mothers who do not give up on our children, even when they turn their backs on us. We are the workers who continue to produce, even when our pay isn't comparable to men's. We are the daughters who take care of aging parents and let our siblings off the hook. We are the girlfriends who are always willing to give our men a second chance.

Time for You

What is it that distinguishes you from the men in your life? Are you more committed to relationships? Are you more driven to receive love?

Do you need to control the love you receive from your relationships?

Women are born with an innate capacity for love that so drives the female soul that, at times, it appears to be the very opposite of love. Since we all want love, how do we find the love our souls are longing for? How do we stop looking for love in all the wrong places?

Learning Where to Look for Love

You won't get anything out of this book unless you develop a love relationship with God. Several years back, I was counseling a young woman who was engaging in premarital sex.

She dismissed her actions with, "All right, I suppose it's wrong, technically speaking. But after all, I have needs. And it's not like I'm not using birth control and safe-sex measures."

As in any therapeutic relationship, my opinion was important to her, and I knew that.

So one day she said to me, "I know you would like me to stop having sex with my fiancé."

"Don't stop having sex to make me happy," I replied. "It's really of no consequence to me whether you have sex with your boyfriend or not. What I long for you to have is a sense of trust in God that His command that you not have sex with your boyfriend is out of love for you."

How many affairs, bankruptcies, depressions, and family problems could be avoided if we lived by this approach? Trying to fill a loveless soul with relationships and things will never satisfy it. If we could only get in touch with how fully and deeply we are loved by our Creator and receive His instruction as founded in His safe and wise affection for us, we could avoid much needless pain and many dead-end journeys.

A Call to Women

If the cycle of damaging relationships won't work, what will? The opposite of this controlling behavior is vulnerable trust in God. In Part Three, we will reveal more of what that means. Now I'd like to lead you along a personal journey as you think about your own lost loves and how they have influenced your identity as a woman. What past rejections need to be scrubbed off the tender recesses of your soul?

CHAPTER SEVEN

Growing Up Female

Before eye color is determined or personality unfolds, before race becomes detectable, even before the single-celled fertilized egg divides, a person's gender has been established. And at the time of birth, it is the one point of reference everyone attributes to a human being. Gender is the initial identity given to a newborn. "It's a girl!" and "It's a boy!" are statements that will shape a child from the first seconds of birth to the grave. Those exuberant shouts will determine a great deal about how a child will be perceived by others and what she will believe about herself.

These perceptions and beliefs are influenced by parents, society, and church. They each contribute to a woman's female identity. Because we don't develop our sexual identity in a vacuum, it is important to look at how these three areas influence how we see ourselves as women.

We have already seen how Regina's feminine identity was influenced by her parents, society, and church. Up to her mid-thirties, she found herself searching for a sense of feminine identity from each of these sources. After she realized the emptiness of her mother's life (parents), she pursued feminism (society). When she became a Christian, she found that even the church and its view of God didn't give her adequate answers. Living the role of a good Christian wife and mother left her unfulfilled.

The way God planned it, women and men would experience their sexual identities (as specifically chosen by Him) in a delicate balance of mutual dependence and unity. God planned for infants to have parents who would demonstrate, as well as nurture, a strong sense of sexual identity as a foundation for healthy self-esteem. He created us to function and live in societies that would encourage distinctive sexual identity in positive, nonoppressive ways. In God's plan, the qualities that make males and females alike and distinct would be valued equally by society.

But since we live in a world uprooted by sin, unhealthy sexual identity is another obstacle that prevents us from being the women God intended us to be. We don't experience life on earth the way God planned it, but we do have the opportunity to experience healthy sexual identity by discovering how God made us. The only sinless human being, Jesus, demonstrated a strong sense of sexual identity.

Luke 2:52 says that Jesus grew in wisdom and stature and in favor with God and man. There is no verse that specifically comments on Jesus' view of Himself as a male. However, His life demonstrates that He had a strong sense of healthy, balanced masculinity. Joseph, Jesus' earthly father, was a carpenter (Matt. 13:55), and Jesus demonstrated an acceptance of and identity with Joseph by performing the same vocation. Further, we observe Jesus having the freedom to follow God's plan for His life and leave the trade of His father to become a teacher and ultimately our Savior. Jesus never defined Himself by a rigid role.

Perhaps the strongest evidence of His healthy sexual identity is the way Jesus treated women. In contrast to the men of His day, He was unusually respectful toward women (Luke 8:1–3). He wasn't threatened by them, nor did He feel a need to put them in their place. A man's oppression of women is rooted in his own insecurity.

Jesus' healthy masculine identity is evidenced even as He was dying on the cross. He did not want to leave His earthly mother without someone to care for her and assigned the task to John (John 19:26–27). Caring for the women of a family was the responsibility of the male head of the household.

Jesus' masculinity was chosen by God. Masculinity was confining to Jesus because in His existence as God, He is not limited to sexuality. However, He accepted that God's purposes for His life on earth involved taking the form of a masculine human being. His parents raised Him as a son, and He functioned in society according to masculine expectations.

We see how Jesus developed a healthy masculine identity in the context of His relationship with His parents (John 19:26), the society and culture in which He lived (Matt. 13:55), and in relation to the God whom He served (Luke 3:22). These same three influences have affected your life and are significant to how you view yourself as a woman.

Parents

For females, the mother is the example of femininity from which the daughter either accepts or rejects her own internalized feminine self. Daughters look to their mothers to learn what femininity is all about. In the normal process of developing female identity, the mother will be rejected during late adolescence. However, during most of the daughter's development of female identity, the mother remains a constant and critical figure for her to process her feelings and beliefs about being a woman. For females, the response to the crises of sexuality are affected significantly by their relationships with their mothers or mother figures.

The father's or father figure's impact on female identity is slightly different. His daughter doesn't look to him as an *example* of femininity; she looks to him for the *value* of her femininity. While the mother provides the role model for femininity, the father gives his daughter permission or approval to be a female. It is in the father's presence that a daughter experiences herself uniquely as a female. Through relationship with a father, a girl begins to learn that her femininity makes her different from him. She learns to feel valued as a female by observing the way her father treats her and other women. His role is critical to communicating the value of femininity, at the same time that the mother demonstrates the ways of femininity.

At first, Regina admired her mom and thought she was perfect. When Regina's mother filed for divorce from her father, Regina distanced herself from both parents. Regina scrutinized her mother the most. She considered her mother a failure, unable to keep her family together. By college, Regina wanted to find an identity totally distinct from her mom's. The best avenue she found at that time was feminism because it was the complete opposite of the life her mother appeared to be living.

Regina's father wasn't very involved in her growing up. Before the divorce, he seemed to emerge only to say she could or could not go somewhere or to praise her if she made good grades. After the divorce, he almost disappeared from her life. He never remembered birthdays or purchased gifts for Christmas. But he did pay every dime of her college education. To Regina, it felt as if her father believed her value was in her ability to perform well at school.

Society

All societies and cultures demonstrate stereotypical gender roles. Usually, the majority of men and women in a society conform to some observable and consistent gender behaviors. Sociologists and anthropologists disagree about the origins of these behavioral differences. The discussion is about whether they are attributed to innate causes (nature) or societal pressure and expectations (nurture).

Women are intuitive about the expectations of others. Part of what held Regina back from responding to the gospel was the dread of what her college peers would think of her. Placing her trust in a masculine God to save her from her sins was very different from putting her trust in herself and discovering her own inner power. But feminism just didn't work for her; it didn't satisfy her soul. Still, she feared that her friends would see her as a Neanderthal woman if she accepted the beliefs of the church.

After college, Regina married. When her first child was born and she quit work, Regina went through another identity crisis. In college, Regina had been indoctrinated to believe that the ability to get and keep a high-paying job and develop a successful career increased a person's value in the eyes of society. Now she had to fight a sense of worthlessness because she had given up her career to be with her child.

A large segment of our society still believes that the only women who are valuable and worthy are those who sever all ties with traditionalism. In my opinion, the radical feminist organization NOW (National Organization for Women) really represents only a select group of women. According to this group, any woman who is against abortion or who believes traditional family values are important is out of touch with reality. But then, I've also talked to mothers with jobs outside the home who sometimes feel judged by the church. It seems you can't win in our society.

Church/View of God

During their early years, boys and girls embrace God with about the same cheery, nongender-oriented élan. It isn't until later in development that a girl begins to really understand herself in relationship to God or the church. Many women in various religions and regions of the world have come to view themselves as second-class citizens because, frankly, they have been taught that God made them that way. For this reason feminists attack religion, seeing the church as a great oppressor of women.

I was brought up in the church and responded to Jesus' invitation to become a Christian at the age of seven. When I was about 10 years old, I remember being in a girls' group at church in which we were discussing what we wanted to be when we grew up. I declared that I wanted to be a pastor. The teachers seemed taken aback by my statement. Even at my tender age, I could sense their dumbfoundedness. (I was raised in a church that didn't ordain women.)

After a few moments, one of them recovered and said, "That is a very good desire. I'm sure the Lord will continue to lead you."

Although I didn't understand until much later what their discomfort was all about, I appreciate the fact that they didn't discourage my honest response.

If you grow up in an oppressive church in which women are considered inferior to men, you can't help but begin to believe that God thinks less of you than He thinks of males. For better or for worse, the "God" figures under whom you grow up give you a strong sense of how you think God views you.

Regina saw God in much the same way as she saw her father—as someone to perform for. After college, she responded to God at a more personal level when she sensed that He did love her because He didn't ask her to perform; rather, He simply wanted her to accept His love through Jesus. However, it wasn't long before she found herself again in a performance role with God and defining herself by that role.

Stages of Development for Healthy Feminine Identity

As our bodies change from helpless infants to full-grown women, our sexual identity expands and influences our overall view of ourselves. A normal healthy process of developing female identity involves several stages. You probably passed through each of these stages without even thinking about how they influenced you. That's why I think it is important to reflect on your life. In doing so, you may identify wrong beliefs you developed about your sexuality that keep you from embracing the healthy feminine identity God offers you.

To help us identify the obstacles to developing a healthy feminine identity, I've broken down our lives into separate stages of development and raised issues at each stage that will guide us in our discussion of how to become the women God intended us to be.

Girlhood

Stage One: Ages 1–2   I am a girl.

Stage Two: Ages 3–5   I want to be like Mommy so Daddy will love me.

Stage Three: Ages 6–10   I want to be like the other girls.

Stage Four: Ages 11–13   I am a woman-girl.

Womanhood

Stage Five: Ages 14–18   I must not be like my mother.

Stage Six: Ages 19–29   I have both male and female characteristics.

Stage Seven: Ages 30–50   I am my mother.

Stage Eight: Ages 50 and Up   I am a woman.

As you read the next two chapters, I want you to think about each of these stages in your own life and identify the influences on your idea of femininity. Chapter 8 will cover the first four stages and focus on girlhood. Chapter 9 will look at womanhood, stages five through eight.

Many women report that they have no memory of childhood. This is common. Sometimes the reason for the repressed memory is that these women do not want to remember one or more traumatic events (such as sexual molestation, an abusive childhood, or exposure to traumatic events, such as the death of someone close or war). They unconsciously erase all memory in an effort to protect themselves from pain.

When I talk to women who have no childhood memories, I suggest that they pray, asking God to reveal to them what they need to remember in order to grow. I have found that this memory lapse allows our brains to protect us from despair and hopelessness. If as an adult you're suicidal, depressed, have an eating disorder, or suffer from other emotional problems, it might be time to consider past issues that may be haunting you in the present.

As you read the next two chapters, reflect on the kinds of messages about yourself you received as a child that may be keeping you from enjoying the freedom God longs for you to have.

CHAPTER EIGHT

The Girl Within

Almost every woman can recall a memory, a place, or a period of her life that represents true girlhood. It is an image of carefree innocence. There was once a time in every woman's life when she had confidence, when she believed that life would give her what she wanted and that all she needed to do was go after it. Even girls raised in dysfunctional and abusive homes can usually remember a time of peace and contentment, a time when they had hope.

For me, these feelings are strongest when I think of visiting my grandfather's house. There I was free to be a girl—running, swimming, playing, laughing. Whatever I was, I was. Maybe your image of girlhood was putting on jewelry in your grandmother's bedroom. Perhaps it was exploring the neighborhood with your favorite dog. Or it could have been baking cookies with your mother. What sights, smells, and senses take you back to that special place called girlhood?

Girlhood is characterized by a time when a child believes that people will always love her, nurture her, and be with her; a time when a girl lives to learn about and explore the world.

At one time, a child is sure that life will be easy and that it will bring her the love she craves. But then, somehow, the carefree, eager enthusiasm of girlhood becomes buried under reality. Day by day, the outgoing, self-confident creature becomes more self-doubting and self-absorbed. How does this happen? What changes her? How can a woman regain the hope of her girlhood?

Those may be difficult questions for some of you to answer. Perhaps the pains of life drown out the memory of any time, any relationship, or any place that seemed carefree. The reason you lost the confidence of girlhood is that as you matured, you had to face the fact that you are a sinner living in a corrupt world. But you can regain this childhood hope as you place your trust in Christ.

Let's look at girlhood stage by stage and discover what *is* and what *is not* a part of a healthy sexual identity at each life passage. Think about yourself at these stages and the people and experiences that influenced you. Try to understand the ways your own feminine identity was blossoming.

Stage One: Ages 1–2— I Am a Girl

When a girl is born, she experiences her first crisis before she is even able to think in abstract forms. A young child encounters the world only in terms of what she can see, feel, hear, smell, and taste. As far as her female identity is concerned, a little girl focuses on whether she is loved and cared for. She receives feedback about whether she is accepted by the way her parents or caregivers respond to her needs. When it comes to sexual identity at this stage, the question is, Can the infant trust that she will receive love and nurture from the caregivers?

An infant child can be born and not loved simply based on sex. I remember a father telling me that when his third daughter was born, a male acquaintance said to him, "I'm sorry you had another girl." My friend interpreted the comment to mean, "Girls just aren't as important as boys." The development of healthy female identity at this stage of a girl's life depends on the parents having a positive view of the child as the sex she is.

If the response of the parents or caregivers to the child's gender isn't positive, the groundwork for an unhealthy identity is laid. Since a child has immature reasoning abilities and is dependent on the feedback received from parents at this stage, it might seem deterministic. However, during adolescence, a girl develops abstract reasoning abilities. At this time, the girl is able to move beyond concrete reasoning, from "My father wanted a son and I am a girl, so I am bad" to "I have felt pressured all my life because it seemed my father was not happy that I was born a girl. It hurts me to know this, but I believe that God created me as a girl and that He is pleased to call me 'daughter.'" She can develop a healthy feminine identity based on the truth of who God says she is.

Diane couldn't remember herself at the ages of one and two. She did know, however, what her mother, aunts, uncles, and others had told her: that her daddy was sorry she wasn't a boy. Diane's parents decided they would have only two children. Diane was the second born; she came after her sister, Jan. Diane's father never expressed any verbal disappointment that Diane was a girl. However, he did relate to her differently from the way he related to Jan. He totally ignored her older sister, but when Diane was old enough, he took her fishing, coached her in sports, and taught her about mechanics. Although Diane didn't remember how she felt about her parents at this stage, she did know that later in life she strongly identified with her father, which included disapproving of her sister and mother. Her attitude prevented her from developing a close relationship with the other females in her family.

Years later, behind the closed doors of the counseling office, Diane revealed that she was concerned about herself because of her attraction to women. She knew the Bible instructed her against homosexuality, but she felt powerless to control her feelings. This contributed to her perceived failure to be an effective mother and was a dominant factor in the breakup of her marriage.

As Diane reflected on her lost femininity in childhood, it helped her to see that some of her homosexual feelings were linked to the lack of a positive, nurturing relationship with her mother and her overidentification with her father. Once Diane saw this and began to grieve the loss and forgive both of her parents, her attraction toward women subsided. Through prayer and confronting these issues, she discovered healing.

Diane realized at a young age that if she wanted her father's love, she would have to do the impossible: change her sex. Since she did not have access to that kind of medical technology, she changed her sex in every way she could. She became Daddy's little boy. She began to do the things Daddy did, such as working on cars and fishing, and she dressed and acted like a boy.

It is not wrong for girls to help their fathers work on cars or do things that their fathers like to do. In fact, it helps develop a well-rounded individual. However, Diane wasn't just enjoying time with her daddy; she was learning that it was bad to be a girl and she could only be significant in relationships if she were a boy.

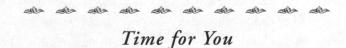

Time for You

How do you think your parents felt about you as a girl?

A healthy feminine identity for a young child at Stage One is exhibited as she is appropriately attached to her parents or caregivers. This means that a child has opportunities to be loved—held, fed, and nurtured—by both her mother and her father. This lays the foundation for the child to believe that she is loved for who she is.

Stage Two: Ages 3–5— I Want to Be Like Mommy

Again, at this stage the mother is the example of femaleness that the daughter will reject or reflect. In a healthy mother-daughter relationship, the daughter will begin to imitate her mother in many ways. The father is also important to the daughter at this stage of development because part of the reason the daughter wants to be like Mommy is to get Daddy's approval.

When my daughter, Rachel, was at this stage, no matter what I was doing, she was usually imitating me. She loved to dress up and put on makeup, but most of the time she was pretending to pore over manuscripts, type at the computer, or write a note to God. I was living with the greatest compliment—imitation—every day. Whatever I did, she desired to do, too. If I did something that Brian typically did, she would reprimand me with "That's what Daddy does."

At this stage of development, Rachel found security in knowing there was someone to imitate, someone from whom to learn what femininity is all about. She used me as a point of reference. She had a limited and immature picture of femaleness when she thought that Mommy couldn't fix a broken toy, but already she was beginning to recognize that there are differences between her mother and her father. Her desire was to be given a set of rules to follow to help her become secure in her identity.

For a long time, our society has functioned at this level of maturity in terms of recognizing femaleness and maleness. In the 1950s, we regulated behaviors, vocations, and positions as male or female. In the 1990s, jobs, positions, and roles are not so concretely defined. In a society in which rigid roles are not enforced, Rachel will be able to develop a more complete identity as a woman. She will be freer to follow God's direction for her life and not be restricted to thinking that some vocations are only for men.

Though Diane's parents were married most of her growing-up years, she always felt the tension between them. In a way, there was a battle of the sexes waging in her own home. Whereas most little girls at this stage of development will imitate their mothers, Diane distanced herself from hers. She felt rejected by her mom when her mother looked for opportunities to leave Diane with her father while she and Jan went shopping. It seemed that Jan and her mom could talk openly about anything, while Diane's conversations with her mother were limited to daily chores and instructions. Diane began to think it was the price she had to pay because it seemed her daddy liked Diane better than her sister and mother. Diane never thought her mom had enough love in her heart for both of her daughters. Her parents were too caught up in their own pain and sin to show their children a healthy view of femininity.

Time for You

Who were your male and female role models at this stage?

Briefly describe what kind of role models they were.

During Stage Two, a child begins to experience firsthand that she is a girl and that her interactions with the world are greatly influenced by this fact. From which public rest room to use to what kind of haircut to get, a young child starts to notice many differences between males and females, not the least of which are sexual characteristics.

A girl who manages this stage successfully is able to identify male and female differences without putting more value on one than the other. The preschooler will notice that women wear makeup and men shave their faces, but it doesn't mean one is superior to the other; they are simply different.

Stage Three: Ages 6–10— I Want to Be Like the Other Girls

During this period, children become attached to play partners of the same sex. Also during this stage, male and female differences become segregated in play. Girls learn that they are most accepted and most in control when they are in relationship with other girls. They know how to play with girls, and they like the same toys, games, and experiences. Their more complicated social development and less aggressive nature separate them from boys. This period is foundational for females subconsciously deciphering the differences between themselves and boys. In healthy female development, girls will sometimes include boys in their play and engage them in conversation, because they realize there is something compelling about them. But for girls to function best and maintain the most control in their world, it is necessary for them to unite with others of their sex. It appears to be a way of coping until their identity is more solidified and they can be who they are even in the presence of someone with a different mind-set and nature, such as a boy.

Some girls feel most at ease with boys. At times, this is simply because there are only boys to play with, but often it is from not being comfortable relating to girls. When this happens, strong feminine identity may be stifled. It is important for girls to socialize with others girls in order for them to value their identity as females.

Diane played with boys because she seemed to have more in common with them. Her parents labeled her a tomboy and didn't express much concern about this behavior. Diane was tough on the outside; that's why the boys accepted her. But deep inside, she ached for a relationship with her mom. And yet even at that young age, she probably knew in her innermost being that it would never be possible.

Diane did become friends with a girl one summer while visiting her grandparents. Once when she spent the night at the girl's home, the girl showed Diane how to masturbate. The girl's mother walked in, scolded them harshly, and forbade them to play together. This left Diane completely perplexed about herself. When she was close to girls, she got hurt or shamed. She began to believe that her desire for female relationships was wrong because she seemed to receive the most rejection from women. Also, she felt shamed about her sexuality because of the way her friend's mother had reacted to her. Since no one told her that she was created by God as a sexual being and that there are healthy and unhealthy ways to express her sexuality, Diane didn't understand where she fit or what she was supposed to be.

In general, girls' self-esteem is relatively intact at this stage. As we noted earlier, girlhood is often characterized by hope and adventure. Girls are focused on discovering how they fit in the world and usually don't pick up on definite boundaries until adolescence.

A girl with a healthy sense of self by age 10 will have several girlfriends, share a close relationship with her mother, and enjoy special conversations with her father. She can understand the concept that God loves her, her sin separates her from Him, and Christ's death brings her back into relationship with Him. During Stage Three, a girl is eager to explore the world and discover all the new and exciting opportunities that await her.

Stage Four: Ages 11–13—
I Am a Woman-Girl

My counseling office often overflows with concerned and even frantic parents of 12- to 14-year-old daughters who are petrified for these women-girls. Fathers feel out of control and inadequate to protect their daughters from the dangers of boys, drugs, sex, and so on. Mothers feel rejected by their preteen daughters' fluctuating moods and attitudes.

This stage of becoming a woman creates an eruption in every aspect of a girl's life. Her body is changing; her friends are changing; her relationships with her parents and with boys are changing. She is leaving a carefree world of petty disagreements with girls and casual antagonism toward boys for a world where her worth is partly determined by how appealing she is as a woman.

Even Diane's camaraderie with boys changed when she reached this stage. She knew how to talk to them and how to play with them. But at age 12, when her breasts were beginning to develop and pimples covered her face, the boys seemed too distracted by the fact that she was a girl to see her the way they once had. Diane found herself feeling rejected and abandoned. When she was around the guys, she laughed off their comments about her and other girls' bodies, and she appeared cool when a male friend made fun of her pimply face. But inside, she was becoming more confused about what her life was supposed to be. Her dad even became more distant. Diane felt that her developing breasts offended him somehow, and that he just couldn't bear to look at her anymore because she was a woman.

Ages 11–13 are the years in which we make significant decisions about what our lives as women will involve. Diane decided that her life was doomed to loneliness and isolation. She felt unwanted by her mother and sister, her father, and her old gang, the neighborhood boys. So she retreated to a world of books. She found that teachers approved of her eager efforts to learn. Being smart and knowing all the answers was a way to belong in an otherwise confusing and uninviting world. Deciding that relationships were too difficult to deal with, Diane determined that she would exist to perform. She cut herself off from the part of her soul that longed for intimacy and acceptance.

Lovely Joy, on the other hand, barely went through an ugly stage. Her mother was extremely good at covering any awkwardness with charm school and dainty clothes. At this stage, Joy found that her status with girlfriends changed: Instead of being the most popular, she became the most envied. Even so, Joy never lacked for female companionship. She always had at least one friend who wanted to be cool by associating with her. But even in her early teens, Joy sensed that she had to play her cards just right. To these fair-weather friends, she dared not reveal too much of herself because her current best friend probably would not hesitate to stab her in the back by humiliating her or giving away a secret.

Toying with boys' affection became Joy's greatest preoccupation. That seemed to be what she did best. Guys were willing to do almost anything for her. Joy found a power in womanhood that she had never felt before. Except for the envy of some of the girls, she began to believe she had life under control.

෴ ෴ ෴ ෴ ෴ ෴ ෴ ෴ ෴ ෴

Time for You

Who was your best friend during this stage?

What were you like during these years of storm and crisis?

What was your relationship with your parents like?

How did you feel about your changing (or not changing) body?

How did boys begin to treat you?

෴ ෴ ෴ ෴ ෴ ෴ ෴ ෴ ෴ ෴

Symptoms of a healthy passage through Stage Four of feminine sexual development are a young woman's acceptance that her life has changed and her willingness to take greater responsibility for her own thoughts and actions. The change she must accept is the fact that she is no longer a child. Her budding sexuality causes a radical shift in her view of herself, boys, and adults. She needs to begin to control emerging sexual feelings. She needs to come to terms with rules she received from her parents, school, and church. She needs to recognize that the influence of her peers is becoming more important to her. During this stage, a girl begins to lose her innocence and her belief that the world was designed to bring her happiness. She learns to accept that conflicting emotions, opinions, and actions are a part of her struggle to develop her own identity. A strong feminine identity is exhibited as the preteen recognizes her differences but does not see them as flaws and does not allow her femininity to hold her back.

Now that we've examined the stages of our girlhood, let's move on to womanhood, beginning with those confusing and treacherous years when we first began the transition from being girls to becoming women.

$\mathscr{B}$ecoming a Woman

I was 28 years old when the Ivana and Donald Trump story was the news of the day. I remember hearing a quote by Ivana in which she said she planned to look 28 forever. It made me stop and think, *What is so great about being 28?*

Whatever stage of womanhood we are in, there are always exciting, challenging, and painful realities to face. It's when we stop moving forward, stop recovering from the crises (e.g., lost employment, parenting disappointments, intrusive relatives), and stop grieving our losses (e.g., the breakup of a marriage, the death of a parent, a miscarriage) that we get stuck with a shallow definition of feminine identity. Like Ivana, we'll think femininity is what we look like or how many Bible studies we have done or how much we can accomplish. This keeps us searching for fulfillment in the wrong ways, which leads only to despair. It's like aimlessly drifting away from home.

Becoming a woman physically begins for some girls as early as 10 or 11. The female body develops a form that is simultaneously ridiculed, worshiped, and lusted after. The most objectified symbol of womanhood is breasts. Breasts are constantly displayed on billboards and TV and in movies and magazines. There are even bars and restaurants that draw customers through the display of women's breasts.

A friend told me about a women's luncheon she attended. The guest speaker, a male doctor, made this his opening statement: "Ladies, I want to talk to you today about the center of your female identity—your breasts."

Outraged, my friend stood up and roared, "My breasts are not the center of my female identity!"

I spoke with another young woman who developed breast cancer after having her breasts enlarged during her adolescence. She had to have a double mastectomy to save her life. One day she was reading a bra advertisement that promised women, "Keep your original shape." My friend wept, wondering, "What is my original shape?"

The pressure to conform to an ideal form of womanhood is a strong underlying current in our society and culture. At the same time that our bodies are taking on the shape of womanhood, our souls are subconsciously developing a core belief from media, society, family, and peers about what it means to be a woman.

Satan would love for us to base our identity on the size and power of our breasts. He knows this will lead us right to the place he wants us to be: pathetic, shamed, and unhappy. As a girl becomes a woman, she not only develops breasts, but she also develops a sense of feminine identity. We became the women we are today as we experienced our impact on others during these next stages of life. Words spoken to us and our reactions to them became critical events that led us to how we view ourselves and what we think God thinks of us.

God longs for each of us to develop into a woman not only physically but also emotionally, with confidence and a strong sense of identity. He boldly tells us in Romans 8:29 that He predestined us to grow into the form and likeness of Jesus Himself. Even in a fallen world, we are in the process of becoming the women God longs for us to be. We were each designed to reflect our Creator in unique ways that glorify Him and give us peace.

So why don't we have confidence as women? Because we have all experienced painful events and relationships that have led us to speculate that we may not be worth much. The truth is that we are women made in God's image. If we really believed and lived this truth, we would have a confidence that defies worldly reason. For even if we aren't especially talented, rich, famous, or beautiful, we are His. Lasting confidence is developed through relationship with God and leads to a life that no longer clings to abilities, fame, possessions, or beauty. We need to stop looking in the wrong places to find fulfillment and happiness. When stripped of worldly things, we are left to look within ourselves, and there, with the right light, discover that it is relationship with God that soothes a hurting soul.

God's hope for us is that we develop into confident women through our relationship with Jesus Christ. In Ephesians 3:11–12, we are told, "This was in accordance with the eternal purpose which He carried out in Christ Jesus our Lord, in whom we have boldness and confident access through faith in Him."

Are you a confident woman? If your answer is "no" or "not very," think through your experiences during the stages of womanhood.

Stage Five: Ages 14–18— I Must Not Be Like My Mother

I remember my mother telling me when I was in my twenties that after the conflicts we experienced during my adolescence, she thought I would never like her again. Every healthy girl rebels to some degree. If a mother or father is too enmeshed or too controlling with a daughter, it prohibits separation and hinders the daughter's maturity. At Stage Five, it is healthy for girls to take a long, close look at their mothers and decide to form their own ideal of womanhood. An adolescent girl's major task is to develop a sense of identity apart from those of her parents. She makes a conscious decision to become different from them.

Faye was typically rebellious as a teenager. In her determination not to be like her parents, she put herself in dangerous situations. Because she liked to be popular, she followed the crowd. At 15 she began drinking, never admitting, of course, that she actually hated the taste of beer. Since she always held back more than her friends did, she figured she could handle anything—until the party at the cabin.

It began the way most parties did. Telling her mom that she was spending the night with her best friend, Faye joined a group at a cabin in the mountains. Faye's friend Kim had invited some guys from a different school, and she wanted Faye to meet them. They were dazzlers, especially Rob, a good-looking football player who took a shine to Faye. They became a twosome almost immediately as they drank a few beers and laughed with the others. When Rob spirited Faye away to the bedroom, she thought they were just going to fool around a little. Faye was a virgin and planned to stay that way. But Rob was smooth, and before long he had persuaded her to take her clothes off.

Pushing her onto the bed, Rob rolled over on top of her. Trying to remain sophisticated, Faye struggled to get away, insisting that she needed to go. Rob pushed her back and ignored her "No! Stop!" It was over in just a few minutes.

Faye lay there, devastated. She loathed herself. She couldn't believe she had lost her virginity to a stranger. Trembling, she got dressed and tried to put the whole terrible experience out of her mind. It wouldn't go away, of course.

Rob left the party, and Faye made up an excuse to Kim that she was sick and needed to be by herself. No one ever found out what happened that night. Faye was too ashamed to tell anyone.

For the longest time, Faye tried to deny that the rape had ever happened. But deep down, the truth never left her. She always believed that she was worthless and damaged somehow because she wasn't able to handle that important situation. She never saw Rob again, but every time she looked in the mirror she saw the face of a tainted woman. The worse she felt about herself, the harder she worked to please others. People, particularly her parents and teachers, praised her efforts to be more serious and responsible.

After graduating from college, Faye married Jack, a high school dropout and chronically out-of-work auto mechanic. Subconsciously, Faye believed that because she had been so bad, Jack was the only kind of man she deserved. She knew, deep inside, that she was not the paragon everyone thought she was.

Diane, on the other hand, continued along the same rigid path she had begun in preadolescence. She focused on pleasing teachers and making good grades. Though she occasionally dated, basically she was viewed as a no-nonsense girl who had no time for parties or drinking. Most parents of rebellious adolescents would have considered Diane to be the ideal teenager.

On a deeper level, Diane was indeed rebelling, and the target was her estranged parents. She began to envision herself as a successful lawyer who would never again need her small-town family. She would satisfy the hunger inside her with the fruits of her successes. She rejected the values and lifestyle of her stay-at-home mom and shoe-salesman dad and determined that her world would be completely different from theirs.

Diane's rebellion was healthy in some ways because she was beginning to see that she could make individual choices about the woman she wanted to be. She was able to see herself as different from her parents and as possessing the ability to make decisions for herself.

Faye's rebellion, however, left her with only negative consequences. The rape and her subsequent self-loathing squelched any desire to pursue her own individuality. Afraid of making decisions for herself, she retreated into the security of her parents' opinions.

Time for You

Did you rebel against your parents at this stage?

In what way were you most determined not to become like your mother?

What kinds of experiences did you have with boys, and how did they affect how you saw yourself at this stage?

A girl with a healthy feminine identity at Stage Five will emerge from an overidentification with her family to a separate and confident individual identity. She will be able to see where she begins and where her parents end. She will also be able to respect her parents, even if her values and morals differ from theirs.

Stage Six: Ages 19–29—
I Have Both Male and Female
Characteristics

By this stage, a healthy woman has developed confidence in her sexual identity. She has become more comfortable in her womanly form. In her confidence, she becomes willing to step out of roles and peer definitions to discover who she really is. She observes both male and female characteristics in her personality and develops strengths in both areas. It is during this stage that most women make the two most important decisions of their lives: whom they will marry and what their vocations will be.

In college, Diane remained focused and goal oriented. She received a B.A. in history and became the youngest student at her law school. She rarely dated as an undergraduate, but by the time she entered law school, she was beginning to loosen up. That's when Tim entered her life. They met in the university law library. Tim was two years older than Diane and beginning his third year. Undeterred by the cold shoulder Diane habitually gave men who seemed interested in her, Tim took each rebuff as a reason to try harder.

Diane marveled at his persistence. "Can this guy take rejection, or what?"

Eventually, Tim won Diane over, and the two began to date. Their relationship waxed hot and cold all through law school. The summer Tim graduated, Diane's persistent coolness began to give him second thoughts. He worked past them, though, when she confided that she had a hard time with intimacy but she really did love him. Now, Tim thought, they were getting somewhere. They were finally communicating.

They married when Diane finished law school, postponing their honeymoon until after she completed her bar exam. Distracted and anxious about the wedding preparations and exam, Diane was a bit forgetful about her birth control measures. The couple found themselves expecting a baby within the first three months of marriage.

Tim knew Diane didn't want children, but when he heard she was pregnant, he couldn't hide his happiness. Diane mistook Tim's attitude for control and thought he had planned it this way. She was determined to build a career, no matter what (remember the baggage she was carrying from childhood!), so she signed on with a law firm and found a posh child-care facility for their six-week-old son. Needless to say, none of this contributed to a close and meaningful union between the newlyweds.

Unhealthy feminine identity is defining yourself by a career or a relationship. In Diane's case, she *was* her career.

Faye defined herself by her relationships. Though her parents disapproved and her friends advised her against it, Faye insisted on marrying Jack, the high school dropout. By trying to save Jack from his indolence, Faye wouldn't have to focus on her own perceived shortcomings. Jack wanted Faye because she was intelligent and beautiful and made him look good. And of course, she was also a dandy meal ticket to tide him over between jobs.

Time for You

Did you find that your image of yourself as a woman further developed during your young adult years? In what ways? How did you view yourself?

How did marriage or vocation influence your image of yourself as a woman?

Unlike Diane and Faye, Regina didn't define herself by a vocation or a relationship. When she met Mike at church, it wasn't love at first sight. But she liked him and accepted his invitations for dates. She honestly sought God's opinion about who or if she should marry, and she felt Him directing her to marry Mike. Regina married Mike for companionship, to build a marriage founded on God's love, and to further develop as a person. When they lit the unity candle at their wedding, she requested that neither of them blow their individual candles out, symbolizing that, though one, they were still separate people.

After marriage, Regina realized she was much better at balancing the checkbook, taking care of the lawn, and fixing broken appliances than Mike was. Also, she was happy to encourage Mike's enjoyment of cooking and didn't feel threatened that he was much better at it than she was.

When she had her first child, Regina decided to stay home with the baby even though she enjoyed her career. She had confidence (though she wavered at times) that being with her children was the best thing for her and them.

Regina is an example of a woman with a healthy female identity. She didn't define herself by her vocation, relationships, or a rigid role. She was able to celebrate her uniqueness and understand the deep love God had for her.

Stage Seven: Ages 30–50— I Am My Mother

During this stage of womanhood, we begin to understand our unique gifts and influences on the world. When we don't run from our femininity but truly value it and ourselves, we discover how we are equipped differently from men to make the greatest impact on our world.

Between the ages of 30 and 50, we are challenged to evaluate ourselves in a new way because when we look in the mirror, we are often literally looking into the faces of our mothers. For most of us, the earliest memories we have of our mothers began when they were about these ages themselves. Their identity and ways of life subtly influenced us, even when we found ourselves separated from them by distance or death.

Nobody could have felt more distant from her mother than Diane. When her mother offered to come out and help her with the new baby, Diane declined the invitation and handled it herself. She managed to arrange her mother's and father's separate visits to meet their first grandchild but engineered them to be brief, obliging her to only barely fulfill her daughterly duty.

Diane was so unsure of herself as a woman, a person, a mother, and a wife that she distanced herself more and more from her husband as well. She couldn't talk to Tim about her fears and insecurities, so she turned her shame about herself into anger at him. After all, he had gotten her into this position of uncertainty by marrying her and getting her pregnant. With both of them pursuing demanding careers, there wasn't much family time, and when they did get together, they fought bitterly. Diane was the one to file for divorce. Perhaps she saw it coming in Tim's eyes and wanted to have the upper hand.

Diane was determined not to be the kind of person her mother was. So why was she divorced from her husband and distant from her two children? It seemed she had indeed become like her mother.

Time for You

When did you first realize that you are like your mother in certain ways?

How has your mother influenced your life positively or negatively?

Let's face it: Though in many ways we will be like our mothers, we're also different. Some of the similarities and differences have their origins in our brains and genetic makeup; others have been formed in us through the teaching of social graces handed down to us through the generations. A healthy identity at this stage is one in which we use our feminine strengths to make the world a better place.

Stage Eight: Ages 50 and Up—
I Am a Woman

By the time we've reached these later years, a dynamic sense of wisdom about womanhood is possible. We can achieve an acceptance and understanding of womanhood that only occur through time. Aging brings women to a better outlook and perspective on life in general and on womanhood in particular. Not every woman who turns 50, 60, or 70 will instantly be cured of her poor identity. But women who do reach this stage of life and still recognize their unique contributions to the human race are the ones who demonstrate healthy female identity.

Barbara Bush is a good example of this. When George Bush was running for president for the first time, comparisons were made between his elderly looking wife and the youthful-looking Nancy Reagan. Barbara was advised to dye her white hair, lose a few pounds, and dress more elegantly. With grace and dignity, she ignored the comments and didn't change one aspect of her appearance. She was secure enough in her identity to realize that her value comes from within, not from without. She retained her identity and showed us what true beauty is.

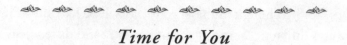

Time for You

What are you continuing to contribute to the world at this stage of life?

What do you hope to be doing 10 years from now?

A woman with a healthy feminine identity at this stage will thoroughly enjoy life, despite our society's view that an older woman doesn't have much value. In fact, she may have even less social value than a stay-at-home mother because she is no longer able to reproduce children. A woman who has a strong sense of identity when she enters middle age will see menopause as an accomplishment rather than a loss; she will also develop a brighter vision of who God wants her to become in the years remaining to her because she will know that as long as she is on this earth, God has a purpose for her. A woman with a healthy feminine identity at this stage lives with confidence that she is deeply loved and deeply valuable to God and others.

Confidence, Not Condemnation

Regina's friend Mary Ellen attended a growth group one evening. Regina wanted Judy, Sharon, Joy, Diane, Brenda, and Faye to meet this 85-year-old jewel.

To hear Mary Ellen talk about Jesus, you might wonder if you were eavesdropping on a conversation from heaven—Jesus was so dear to her. Clearly, He was as intimate to her as any human being. Regina asked her about her marriage and service to the Lord. Mary Ellen talked eloquently about a joyful adventure, making everyday situations—such as taking a walk with her husband, Fred, and encouraging a neighbor—seem like heroic accomplishments.

When she spoke of marriage, Mary Ellen had dynamic memories of a man so faithful and strong that just the mention of his name filled her eyes with tears. She told about the way he comforted her when they lost their son in the Vietnam War. Without denying the adjustments and difficulties in developing a growing marriage, her words left all the married women there appreciating their husbands a little bit more.

Sharon was the one who asked her what she looked forward to most about heaven. Sharon assumed she would say, "Seeing Fred again." But Mary Ellen's response was "Seeing my Jesus face to face." Tears flowed down her cheeks.

Mary Ellen held those women captive, describing the complexity of her life and what a joy it had been to live it. At her age, she couldn't get out much anymore, but she could pray and encourage others. Mary Ellen was the first person the pastor called when he had an urgent prayer need. She was always eager to drop to her knees to intercede on someone's behalf.

The closer we come to God, the more confident we are in who He made us to be and the more willing we are to think less of what people say about us. Most of us don't experience the confidence God wants us to have because we are too busy trying to control our lives and relationships in order to cover our fears and anxieties. We're seeking our security in the wrong areas.

Henry Drummond, an eighteenth-century preacher, said, "Life is the cradle of eternity."[1] This is comforting to me. In my own development into the mature and confident woman God created me to be, I often seem to stride forward only to tumble backward without a moment's notice. Just when I think I'm on my way, my failures bring me back to reality. But God offers us a solution: He asks us to turn away from the tumult of the world and find our peace and security in Him. Like Regina and Mary Ellen, I've noticed that the closer I get to God, the more my soul is anchored in the true Source of my identity and the more I become the woman God intended me to be.

What path will bring us closer to God? Part Three will take us there.

PART THREE

The Source of Our True Identity

CHAPTER TEN

ℋ Love Relationship with God

Our basset hound, Happy, lives in a fenced-off part of our backyard. Every time someone walks down the alley by the fence (which is often), Happy jumps up, barks incessantly, and runs in circles. It didn't take long for him to wear a path in the grass. It is a path that leads nowhere but is well traveled nonetheless. This story is a good example of what we do when we're caught in the cycle of damaging relationships.

How do we get off this dead-end path? First, we must want to get off. Once we've made that decision, we see that there are seven stepping-stones that lead away from the cycle of damaging relationships. In the next few chapters, we will walk together on each of these stones as we take a new path toward freedom.

The first stepping-stone is *developing a love relationship with God*. It's not only our first step away from the cycle of damaging relationships, but it also provides the firm foundation we need to confidently leave the path we know so well. The next stepping-stone is *forgiveness*. Once we're fully assured of God's love, we can break free of the grasp of hurtful relationships by receiving the healing ointment of His forgiveness. After healing from our damaged relationships, we're ready to take the next step. Looking ahead, however, we stop in mid step as we realize we're heading into unknown territory. After running in circles thousands of times, we've become secure in knowing what to expect. Now we must trust that God will watch out for us and keep us safe. Thus, the third stepping-stone is *giving God control,* and it's indispensable if we are to keep moving forward.

The fourth stepping-stone is *practicing spirituality.* Herein lie the spiritual disciplines, the liturgy, and the rituals that bring you closer to God when they are exercised with a healthy heart.

The next stepping-stone is *understanding men.* As we grasp our truest sense of feminine identity, we will be able to help men in grasping their identity. Closely related to the fifth stepping-stone is the sixth—*finding freedom in our sexuality.* This stepping-stone is important as we seek to understand ourselves better and live more abundantly in this world.

Our last stepping-stone is *knowing God.* Each of the previous steps has been a part of this last stepping-stone. As we look at our lives and what the Bible tells us about our unique womanhood, we should finally be able to grasp the true essence of who God created us to be.

The seven stepping-stones lead us to the edge of a garden. Beautiful flowers and overgrown shrubs block our view of what lies before us. This is where we each head in a different and unique direction. Once we know God, we know who we are; then our paths become the process of receiving His answer to "Why am *I* here?" Your path will take you to people I will never meet and to places I will never go, and vice versa. Though at times our paths may cross, no two paths will be exactly the same.

Before you decide whether to take your path, make sure you count the cost. Jesus warned His disciples to do this in Luke

14:26–35. Oswald Chambers described the journey and its cost this way:

Living a life of faith means never knowing where you are being led. But it does mean loving and knowing the One who is leading. It is literally a life of faith, not of understanding and reason—a life of knowing Him who calls us to go. Faith is rooted in the knowledge of a Person.[1]

For me the journey is worth the risks and much better than running in circles. Moving off the cycle of damaging relationships looks like this.

Moving Off the Cycle of Damaging Relationships

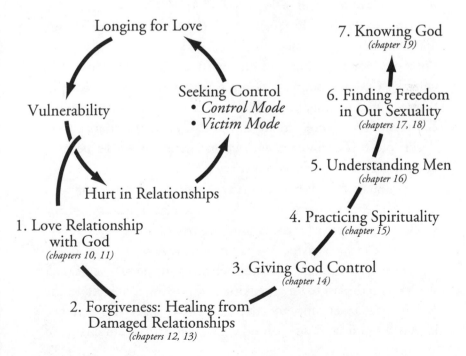

Longing for Love

7. Knowing God
(chapter 19)

Vulnerability

Seeking Control
• *Control Mode*
• *Victim Mode*

6. Finding Freedom in Our Sexuality
(chapters 17, 18)

5. Understanding Men
(chapter 16)

Hurt in Relationships

1. Love Relationship with God
(chapters 10, 11)

4. Practicing Spirituality
(chapter 15)

3. Giving God Control
(chapter 14)

2. Forgiveness: Healing from Damaged Relationships
(chapters 12, 13)

When God Is Not on Our Map

For the past five decades, American women have observed one of Hollywood's most acclaimed females marry, remarry, and marry again. Although we may envy her, try to ignore her, or condemn her, each of us is like her in some way. She is Elizabeth Taylor.

"How," you may ask, "am I like Elizabeth Taylor?"

Few of us have chosen so many, shall we say, interesting and unlikely husbands, but each of us has searched for love and purpose from unlikely, often foolish sources. Most of us, like Elizabeth, have repeatedly followed a path that led us to divorce, dead-end relationships, and emotional destitution (anxiety, depression, despair). We try to convince ourselves through our intimate relationships that we are OK. We are desperately seeking to draw meaning and purpose from empty wells that never satisfy the thirst in our souls to love and be loved (Jer. 2:13).

A lot of us, like Elizabeth Taylor, keep expecting beauty, approval, and men to help us feel loved and wanted. We rarely think of God as the source of the love our souls crave. Most of us consider God as a Supreme Being to be obeyed, a stern disciplinarian with scowling, bushy brows. A loving parent, a satisfying companion, a devoted friend are not ways we experience God during our first encounters with Him. These divine roles become evident only with increased intimacy.

This was certainly the case for Sharon. After becoming a Christian, she followed God's Word to the best of her ability. She was the first to arrive for the evening women's Bible study. She was great in leadership activities such as making announcements, opening prayer sessions, and planning retreats and special events. But she was also the last to leave, making sure the dishes were done, the garbage was taken out, and the chairs were stacked before she locked the church doors behind her. When she was in charge of the women's retreat, everyone raved about the speaker, decorations, location, and every other detail.

During those days, she would have said that she loved God, and no one would have argued with her. But recently she came to realize that she couldn't have loved God because she had never gotten to know Him. She had been so busy serving God that she had never had time to experience a relationship with Him.

God Is Love

Who put the longing for love in our souls? Remember that the originating point on the cycle of damaging relationship is "longing for love." Why are we all born into this world with such a longing? Because God created us in His image, and a significant component of that image is a desire to love and be loved.

God would never allow us to be born with a need without providing for it. In fact, He is the only one who can truly satisfy our love need. First John 4:8 says that "God is love." God defines Himself as love. Again, in 1 John 4:19, we are told that "we love, because He first loved us." God has done everything possible to provide for our love need, though this is sometimes hard for us to see. Our deepest need for love has been provided by God through Jesus Christ. "In this is love, not that we loved God, but that He loved us and sent His Son to be the propitiation for our sins" (1 John 4:10).

There is nothing God wants more than for us to respond to His love. Second Peter 3:9 says, "The Lord is not slow about His promise, as some count slowness, but is patient toward you, not wishing for any to perish but for all to come to repentance."

God desires a relationship with us because He loves us. And He knows that when we respond to His love for us and begin to love Him back by trusting His Word and doing as He wants, we will find soul contentment. Some of us will find financial success;

some, fame; others, health and long life. These are all nice benefits, and they are certainly God-given. But they aren't guaranteed for every child of God. What God promises each one of us, and what cannot be taken away, is a soul linked to Him through love.

In Luke 3:22, God pronounces to the world His pleasure in Jesus with these words: "Thou art My beloved Son, in Thee I am well-pleased." He feels the same about you and me. We are His beloved daughters. We are a precious part of His universe, a part He cannot bear to be without.

What would make you run into your house if you arrived to find it consumed by flames? I have some nice things I really enjoy, but not one would be worth risking my life for. The only reason I would run into a burning house is to save my children. That is how God feels about us. The outcome of Adam and Eve's sin sparked the most hideous devastation any home has ever withstood. But God keeps running back in, listening earnestly for anyone who cries out to Him. Why does He do this? Because we serve Him, love Him, or obey Him? No, because He loves us. In God's opinion, we are worth dying for.

We know about God, and we can accept that our souls crave love. But God and love together is often a difficult truth for us to grasp. We might be able to accept it intellectually, but how many people are deeply assured of God's love for them?

Diane's eyes never left my face as I described God's unconditional love for her. But her blank expression alerted me that she had absolutely no idea what I was talking about. The words I used sounded nice, and in her mind she accepted what I was saying as true. In fact, she offered no argument, and for a lawyer that's something.

Finally, I asked her, "Who has loved you as unconditionally as God does?"

"Nobody," was her reply.

Because she had never experienced a relationship of unconditional love, she couldn't comprehend God's love for her.

Diane had grown skeptical from the rejection she had received most of her life. Any attempt she had made at intimacy had been rebuffed. Now, performance—that is something she could understand. If I offered her rituals to demonstrate her love for God, she would be eager to participate. The whole idea of being loved just because you are, just because you breathe—that was inconceivable to her. For Diane, it was actually absurd to even think of God in that way.

Divine Difference

Do you remember your first love? I was a budding teenager when I developed a crush on an older boy. My friends and I would talk to him and his friends on a regular basis. It was the highlight of my weekend if I got a chance to see him. So went my life until the night he invited me out on a real, live date. He actually said he would call me to tell me what time he would pick me up. The next day, my friends and I started planning which outfit and shoes I would wear, what color my nails should be painted, and how I would wear my hair, even though the date was a week away.

I remember how I felt waiting for his call. Every time the phone rang, I wondered if it was he. I couldn't eat. I couldn't sleep.

Finally, the event of the century happened. I went out on the date. It was fun, but it couldn't begin to match the anticipation I had put into it. My teenage heart was pursuing something new. I was after a new way to get the love I craved. I soon found that teenage boys offer only a poor imitation of the love I really wanted.

My love relationship with God has been just the opposite. It has taken me years to discover and accept how deeply the love He offers penetrates the longing in my soul.

I first sensed God was interested in me when I was seven. I was raised in the church and had watched my older brother and sister be baptized. I knew that it was something I would do if I was ever going to have some of the "snacks" they passed around during the service—what everyone else called Communion. The day I heard God's voice inviting me into relationship was just an ordinary day, during a missions conference at our church. For the first time, God helped me understand that He wanted to have a relationship with me but couldn't because of my sin. I realized that my sin separated me from God and that the reason Jesus came to earth and died was to pay the price for my soul. God wanted a relationship with me and made this possible if I would acknowledge my sin and receive Jesus as my Savior. I said yes to God that day in 1969.

From there, I grew to know a lot about God. I even attended a Christian school where I learned a great deal about the Bible. But I wasn't automatically overwhelmed by God's love for me. Instead, I continued to struggle with who I was and how I could satisfy my need for love on my own. I knew my parents loved me, and I drank sparse droplets of love from my teachers, friends, relatives, and others who came into my life. But it was never enough. And being a Christian didn't seem to make my love need go away. Since I continued to experience rejection, avoiding and controlling it became the focus of my life instead of God.

The Problem of Rejection

We each experience rejection from parents, teachers, friends, and even ourselves. We also give rejection, sometimes without even knowing why. In my counseling practice, I notice that the severest blows are linked to emotional problems such as depression, anxiety, eating disorders, marital problems, and sexual problems. No one is immune to rejection, and we all seek to resolve it in the same way: by trying to control it.

Over time, rejection begins to take its toll on our souls. When we disappoint our parents or break up with a boyfriend or have a fight with our best friend, we wonder whether we are lovable. In previous chapters, I have asked you to consider some of the ways you have been rejected at different stages of your life. The more rejection we experience, the more difficult it is for us to believe that we are truly loved to the degree that God loves us.

Judy grew up with a false sense of love. For her, love meant betraying her soul because the love she received was linked to sexual abuse. Love made her feel dirty and horrid because she mistakenly combined the good attention she received from her father and brother with their sexual abuse to define love. When her mother refused to believe that her dad and brother were abusing her, Judy began to blame herself. She decided that she was the bad one and that she deserved it. She began to expect rejection from everyone, including God.

Sharon was the eldest daughter of six children. She received approval from her mom through caring for the younger children, excelling in school and drama, and being an overall great kid whom everyone could count on. Love for Sharon was a contract. It seemed simple and straightforward. If she did the right things, she got love. If she did the wrong things, she got rejection. When she finally realized that she had done everything God wanted her to do and God still didn't reward her, she decided to reject Him before He could reject her.

To Joy, acceptance meant rejecting the core parts of who she was. She believed she was loved, desired, and wanted as long as she was pretty and entertaining. Joy's mother never allowed her to have opinions about such things as how to wear her hair, how to dress, or whether to take piano lessons. When Joy married, she transferred that power to her husband and allowed him to make decisions for her, except about what she would wear. Joy could never figure out how to have opinions without threatening someone else.

Diane grew up without love. She hurt from the rejection she felt from her mother and sister. Though she appeared resilient on the outside, inside she was deeply insecure. This insecurity showed up in her reluctance to form relationships with other girls. Rejection became the center of her life. She developed a belief that she would always be rejected, so she subconsciously wrote a rejection script into her marriage to Tim. She convinced herself she had to be on guard against Tim because if she wasn't, he would try to control or hurt her.

Brenda's negative encounters with her father—when he over-ruled things she wanted, such as a pretty dress or emotional close-ness—sealed her sense of rejectability with men in particular. She subconsciously believed she could never be loved by a man, even while she hinged her happiness on getting married.

Faye's fear of rejection was the reason she couldn't say no to any request. She was always at the mercy of others. Their needs came first, even if she was seething inside from being asked.

Regina knew rejection and continued to feel rejection in her rela-tionships. But because she was anchored in her love relationship with God, the rejection she felt didn't make her lose all sense of her value. She was able to give and receive criticism in a healthy way. Now when people rejected her, she was able to analyze whether there was some-thing wrong in her life that she needed to deal with, or whether others' rejection of her had more to do with their own problems. Regina had found the freedom and courage to evaluate rejection through God's eyes. This is the healthy way of dealing with rejection: taking an honest look at what is being said to you and discovering if there is any truth in it. Because Regina had developed a deeper relationship with God, she was free to look at rejection without having to control it.

Henri Nouwen said, "Self-rejection is the greatest enemy of the spir-itual life, because it contradicts the sacred voice that calls us the 'Beloved.' Being the Beloved expresses the core truth of our existence."[2]

Self-rejection blocks us from enjoying the love God offers us. The voices proclaiming our rejectability drown out the voice that calls us His Beloved.

We all know what self-rejection sounds like. These voices are so quick to tell us what we must do differently to become acceptable even as they chastise us because we are so faulty. We need to be thinner, taller, more assertive, less assertive, happier, richer, more important, a better wife, married by now, a better mother, a more responsible daughter, a more attentive friend.

And then God whispers our names.

His voice is so different from the others. The One who loves our souls, who created us, offers us the only relationship in which we will find the love our souls were made for.

I find it highly significant that He first loves us. He doesn't initiate a relationship with us based on what we do for Him. He initiates a relationship with us because He wants to. He invites us to love Him and return His love because He knows that is what our souls need. When we love Him, we find contentment; we are at peace.

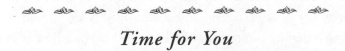

Time for You

How has self-rejection played a part in creating distance in your relationship with God?

How to Receive God's Love

First John 3:1 says, "See how great a love the Father has bestowed upon us, that we should be called children of God; and such we are. For this reason the world does not know us, because it did not know Him."

Oh, if we could only grasp the reality of this, ladies! This is a love that calls us daughters! Repeatedly, God disciplined David, king of Israel. David had every reason to practice self-rejection. And yet, again and again in the psalms, David referred to God as loving and kind. Here was a man who knew God intimately and appreciated His many facets.

Who is God to you? What is your image of Him? Do you know the loving and kind God? Or is He an angry giant in the sky waiting to whip you if He catches you having fun? If we don't know God as love, we don't know Him. I'm not saying that we aren't saved. I'm saying that we, like Sharon, don't have an intimate relationship with Him.

Let's say you know the president—met him (or her!) at a rally and even spent some time in conversation with him. You learn a lot about him during a campaign year, maybe more than you want to know. You read the endless trivia dug up by the media, knowing full well that the favorable items are leaked by the president's camp, and the derogatory ones are leaked by the opposition. You know a lot of it is inaccurate or just plain false, though you don't like to think about that. But there are many things you would not know about your president unless you lived with him. You may not know that he prefers a particular brand of mouthwash or that his favorite story as a child was *Winnie the Pooh*. These are things that only those who are intimate with him know.

When you know God intimately, you will know Him as a loving God. His lovingkindness intertwines the whole of Scripture. When you read Genesis 1–3, you see the love of God poured out.

1. He created man and woman in His own image (Gen. 1:27).

2. He brought animals to Adam before He created woman

so that Adam would realize how special this woman was (Gen. 2:18–20).

3. After Adam and Eve sinned, God came in the cool of the day, as He always had, and called them by name (Gen. 3:8–11). (We don't see an angry, cruel God here.)

4. In the curses, God prepared the man and woman for the painful realities of life outside the garden; that is, man would suffer from fear of inadequacy, and woman would suffer from fear of abandonment (Gen. 3:16–19).

5. God expelled Adam and Eve from the garden because He didn't want them to eat of the tree of life and live eternally in their fallen condition (Gen. 3:22–23).

6. The seed mentioned in the curse to Satan is the promised Messiah (Gen. 3:15).

7. Since fig leaves wouldn't serve well in the world Adam and Eve were entering, God lovingly made them clothing (Gen. 3:21).

This is a picture of a wise, tough, exuberant, determined love.

Though the truth of God's love is clear in Scripture, we still have a difficult time accepting it. Sometimes the distance from the head to the heart is massive. What keeps us from responding to this deep and abiding love?

There is an art to having a mutual love experience with our Creator. His kind of love is literally out of this world. The love or fulfillment we experience from parents, men, success, and fame doesn't come close. There are three resistances we need to overcome in order to prepare our hearts to truly receive God's love. We'll discuss them in the next chapter.

CHAPTER ELEVEN

Steps to Receiving God's Love

The first time I felt God's love in a deep way I was 18 years old and 3,000 miles away from my family and friends. I had been hurt and rejected by a relationship and was preparing to spend the summer ministering to students. I told my parents I would phone them when I arrived at my destination, but because of the time difference and a late-night meeting I had to attend, I missed my chance to call them before they went to bed. I set my alarm for the middle of the night to catch them before they left for work the next morning. My timing was wrong, and I woke them too early. After a short conversation, I said good-bye so they could go back to sleep. Feeling that I had disappointed everyone, I went back to bed.

Completely alone, I lay there, unable to stop my tears of grief. Suddenly, I sensed God's invitation to allow Him to hold me. I distinctly remember turning over in my bed and feeling His arms around me, an assurance that it would be OK. The next morning, I read Psalm 34:18, which says God is close to the brokenhearted. I envisioned Him holding me in His arms, close to His heart. It was the first time I received God's love in the deepest recesses of my soul.

It was similar to the many times I have comforted my children through ear infections, broken bones, or skinned knees. The fact that I am there hugging them does not change the circumstances of their pain, but it does change their perspective on it. Whereas they once felt hurt and alone, they now felt comforted and loved.

If we don't learn how to overcome our deep resistance to God's perfect love, we'll never escape the cycle of damaging relationships. As we consider the three most common ways we resist receiving this love, try to identify the ones that keep you from claiming your belovedness.

Resistance 1—
We Don't Want to Face Ourselves

To paraphrase Luke 7:36–48: "He who is forgiven much is loved much." We can't really experience how much we are loved until we understand how much we have been forgiven. Only when we see ourselves as we really are will we be able to understand the depth of God's love for us. We cannot come into the presence of God without being aware of our sin—which is probably one of the reasons we stay away. The prophet Isaiah said that he saw the Lord high and lifted up. His most immediate reaction to this sight was to call himself a man of unclean lips and say that he lived among a people of unclean lips (Isa. 6:5).

Several years ago, I talked to a teenager who had been rebellious for four years. Instead of receiving the instruction of her Christian parents, she found her own way to enjoy life in high school. On the outside, she appeared to be the daughter they wanted her to be, but behind their backs, she was taking part in the pleasures and entertainment of her friends—definitely not behavior her parents would condone if they knew about it.

Then she got arrested for shoplifting, and her parents brought her to me for counseling. By the time I met with her, however, she had already expressed a sincere desire to be obedient and was trying to put that desire into practice. Her transformation fascinated me.

"What changed?" I asked her. "It's terribly hard to turn your back on friends and a whole way of life. What in the world did your parents do to give you a new sense of direction?"

Her reply: "Now that I know how much they love me, I just don't want to disappoint them anymore."

It turns out that when they came to pick her up at the juvenile hall, her parents' first words were "We love you!" and everything else they said and did backed that up. Their response dumbfounded her. She was willing to drop her friends and begin listening to her parents because of their accepting love. Experiencing her parents' grace changed this young woman's life.

We can't grasp the fullness of God's love until we grasp the fullness of our own sinfulness. But we wholeheartedly resist this because we know that if we see ourselves as we really are, we will want to run and hide, just as Adam and Eve did. As we saw earlier, the sin-shame-blame cycle began in Genesis 3.

The Sin-Shame-Blame Cycle

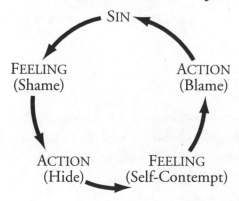

After Adam and Eve had sinned, they felt shame and they responded by sewing fig leaves together in order to conceal themselves. When they realized they couldn't hide from God, their shame turned into self-contempt. To rid themselves of that feeling, they cast blame on God and each other.

Each of us faces a similar dilemma before God. In our sinfulness, we feel shame and self-contempt. Our way of controlling that pain is to crouch in the bushes or point our finger at someone else. God wants us to realize that the only way we're going to be free enough to receive His love is to stand up and admit to Him how broken and needy we are. Only then can He love us the way He wants to.

Picture this. It's Saturday morning, and you're trying to catch up on all those messy jobs you didn't do during the week. You're in your grubbiest clothes, and you smell like a thoroughbred after a race. Your face is covered with grime, and your hair looks like a windswept haystack. You're scrubbing the toilet bowl when you hear the doorbell ring. Muttering under your breath, you swing the door open to find:

• the new pastor and his wife.

• your best friend's mother, who is dying to meet you.

• the person you've just started dating or want to date.

• the head of the PTA.

• [fill in the blank]

Not a pleasant scenario, is it? A person who should be seeing you at your best has found you . . . well, like this instead.

Now let's picture that person waiting to be invited into your house anyway. You hesitate, unwilling to let him or her bask in your uncleanness, as it were. If only you were presentable . . . If only your house were halfway decent . . . If only your toilet weren't foaming blue at the moment . . .

You would expect the person to stammer, "Oh, I see you're busy," and beat a hasty retreat. That's human. And yet, if that someone saw (and smelled!) you at your worst and still wanted to spend time with you, you would be justified in believing that he or she was quite willing to accept you in spite of the mess.

Isn't that what God does? John 14:23 says that if we love Him, we'll obey Him, and He will come and make His home with us. Our hearts are actually home to God. How do you look at your home when you know your mother is coming for a visit? When my mom is coming, all of a sudden I notice the dust on the moldings. It may have been there for a month, but that's the week I do a little extra cleaning. Mom is not critical, and yet I feel a need to get ready for an inspection. After all, she's *Mom!*

God is at home in us in spite of the cobwebs and dirt that we don't see (Jer. 17:9–10). He comes in longing to see us clean up the grime and appear the way He designed us, but He is never unwilling to be there with us, right in the middle of our messes.

This resistance to God's love is rooted in our prior experiences, the many times we have been bruised and broken in our human relationships. Few of us have been seen in all our yuckiness and been loved anyway. When I think about my own relationships, it has been in my relationship with my husband, Brian, that I have been loved most like this. He loves me down and dirty. Brian has seen me at my worst, so his choice to love me penetrates most deeply.

To experience love like that in my human relationships, I must be willing to let myself be known. It is the same with God. Before I can feel enveloped in His love, I first must admit to myself how unworthy I am. But this is something I don't want to think about.

When we won't let ourselves be held in the midst of our messes by the God who loves us and made us, we miss the unspeakable joy of knowing that we are truly His beloved. Jesus paints a picture of God's love for us in the parable of the prodigal son (Luke 15:11–32).

The story's climax is the moment an unaccomplished failure of a son returns home to his father. The father sees him in the distance, runs to him, and embraces him. When we accept that God loves us the way that father loved his son, that no matter how wretched we are, He will wrap His arms tightly around us because He's so glad we've come home, love will begin to flow. That's what our souls long for. That's what our heavenly Father longs to do for us.

To overcome resistance 1, we must allow ourselves to be embraced by God even in the midst of our messes.

Resistance 2—
We Try to Win a Love That Is Freely Given

We are loved, and when we truly love, our love is a response to this reality and not a way to get love. Love that is earned is not love at all. We don't earn God's love. He gives it to us.

Too many Christians become satisfied with their Christian service because it gives them a sense that they are "good enough" before the Father. Susanna Wesley, mother of John and Charles (and 17 other children!) spent her whole life serving God so that He would be proud to have her in heaven. That's how she put it. And if He functioned that way, He certainly would have been proud. Her 10 surviving children left home well educated and knowing right from wrong, and she kept her pastor-husband's parish ministry alive in his many long absences.

Then at the age of 70, as she listened to her son preach, she was what we today would call "born again." For the first time she realized that God is love, not duty; His salvation is a gift, not a salary. When she died at 73, she was at peace with God and with herself.

Relationship with God is about being, not doing. God is more concerned that we be in relationship with Him than that we perform for Him. This is so far from our human experiences, it seems unnatural.

As homework for a Bible study, I was once assigned to take a walk with God. I kept telling myself that I was too busy and put it off. One evening I had a free half-hour while my children were in a meeting at church, so I began to walk around the building. As I walked, I confessed my avoidance of this walk. I talked about how I hadn't done this and that and how I needed to get busy on another project.

Then I distinctly heard God whisper to my heart, *I just want you. I want you to know Me, to love Me, to want to be with Me. All of that other stuff can wait. Come home to Me.*

Why do I feel so drawn to performing for God and overwhelmed by the endless ways I fail? Satan hangs a carrot in front of us and then puts us on a treadmill, telling us this is the only way to show our love for God. Performance is often the only way we've gotten love in human relationships. It is difficult to realize how different divine encounters are from the earthly love we have experienced.

Henri Nouwen said, "I leave home every time I lose faith in the voice that calls me the Beloved and follow the voices that offer a great variety of ways to win the love I so much desire."[1] King David made it clear that the sacrifices God really desires are a broken spirit and a contrite heart (Ps. 51:17). We are never broken or contrite when we are earning love. Just ask Sharon. She was good, and she knew she was good. She just couldn't figure out why God wasn't treating her as if she were good. It wasn't until she stopped being good and admitted that she was angry that she found God. Her anger brought her to brokenness.

God wants our response to His love to be humility, whereas we want to look at all the things we do for Him as the reason He should love us. He wants us to realize that it is He who works in us both to will and do of His good purpose (Phil. 2:13).

Just as an infant smiles and delights his mother, when we smile into the face of our loving Father, we delight Him. All of us want to earn love because this seems to give us more control. Remember how strongly we all—men and women—desire to control. Instinctively, we feel that things beyond control are too scary. This is nothing new. The book of Galatians was written to a whole church that acted this way. Galatians 3:1–3 says, "You foolish Galatians, who has bewitched you, before whose eyes Jesus Christ was publicly portrayed as crucified? This is the only thing I want to find out from you: did you receive the Spirit by the works of the Law, or by hearing with faith? Are you so foolish? Having begun by the Spirit, are you now being perfected by the flesh?"

I must confess that too many things that I've done in the name of loving God have nothing at all to do with loving Him. Rather, they are my feeble attempts to prove myself *worthy* of His love.

What happens to you when someone shows you kindness? Do you want to slap that person in the face? No, you want to return the favor by being kind. When you feel loved by God, you will want to love Him back by serving Him.

We are given a great example of this in John 12:3. A woman came to Jesus and anointed Him with costly perfume and washed His feet with her tears. This wasn't an effort to earn love. Her behavior was motivated by a heart so moved by His love for her that this was the best way she could express the joy in her soul. It was a completely selfless expression. She wasn't saying, "Notice me! I'm doing a good thing for You." She was saying, "Thank You! I feel so loved by You that I want to return that love."

To overcome resistance 2, we must bask in the reality of God's love and see our service and obedience as nothing but the natural outpouring of a soul that is deeply loved.

Resistance 3— We Fear the Unknown

First John 4:18 says, "There is no fear in love; but perfect love casts out fear, because fear involves punishment, and the one who fears is not perfected in love."

Some of our fears are not neurotic—our fear of rejection, for instance. We are rejectable even to God; but if we believe His love story to us and receive His Son as Savior, our fear is unfounded. Fear is completely inconsistent with love. Most people assume that the opposite of love is hate, but actually the opposite of love is fear. People who hate still have a passionate link in the relationship.

We are afraid to love the way God does because it is so foreign to us. We know the rules of conditional love: "If I behave in a certain way, I will be loved." God asks us to come to Him in faith, believing that He is a loving God even though some of the realities on earth don't feel good or comfortable. We want a God who gives immediate rewards. Our God asks us to trust Him to lead us and guide us, even when the path seems frightening and not the way we would have chosen to go. There are a lot of unknowns when it comes to God. The Beatitudes (Matt. 5:3–12) are rich with seeming absurdities, such as loving enemies and forgiving offenders. Hebrews 11:6 says that without faith, it is impossible to please God. We are asked to believe not only that God exists, but also that He rewards those who seek Him.

We deeply resist not having a pseudo sense of control in our lives. I say "pseudo" because our fear of the unknown stems from the fact that we think we can control this world. But can we really?

Judy thought she could control her death when she was 17. Her suicide attempt wasn't a means of getting attention. She *wanted* to die. But God didn't allow her to. I heard a preacher say once that life on earth is like riding mules: We think we are in control, but life is stubborn and often takes us places we would rather not go.

To overcome resistance 3, we must enter fully into God's embrace so that our fears melt away. It is only in believing that we are loved with an everlasting love that we begin to leave our fears behind and experience great joy at the thought of getting to know our Creator better.

Learning How to Receive God's Love

1. Identify Your Image of God

Louis Evely, a French priest, said, "Everyone has his own preconceived notion of God, which nothing can change, but that, too, we must give up—that, before all else."[2]

The image of God I had as a teenager was of a mean, old man in the sky with a whip. As I grew to know Him and experience Him through the pain and tragedies in my life, I began to see Him as the One who held me close to His heart. I felt totally enveloped in His presence, like being consumed by a warm, comforting cloud.

It was gratifying to watch my husband's relationship with God be transformed as he confronted his negative image of the Father. A friend asked him to describe the image of God he held in his mind as he prayed. Brian saw himself standing partway up a big stairway that led to God's throne. Instead of looking toward the throne, Brian was looking down the staircase from where he had come. Aha! With the friend's help, Brian let this image reveal to him his fearful, cautious attitude toward God. It became the catalyst for Brian to develop a healthier view of Him.

God, through the Holy Spirit in His Word, interceded here, of course. God invited Brian up the stairs by overwhelming him with the awesome reality of Hebrews 7:25, which says that Christ constantly intercedes for him, for Brian. While Brian was praying, God allowed him to clearly see and experience this reality. Brian found a wonderful new peace and confidence as he realized that sitting on the throne at the top of the stairway was not only an awesome God but also a loving Savior tenderly expressing Brian's urgent needs to God. Brian was privileged to see Jesus whispering his name, telling God how much He loves him as he came close to the throne.

God is a just, loving, all-powerful, all-knowing healer, ruler, friend, and guide. He uses numerous characteristics to describe Himself in Scripture. We need to face and release our unhealthy views of God before we can receive Him as He truly is.

Time for You

Do you need help breaking through your mistaken image of God? Ask God to reveal to you how He really is.

2. Open Yourself Up to God's Love and Forgiveness

As you complete step 1, you enter into a relationship with God and come to experience His love as you fellowship with Him. You have already opened yourself up when you recognize your sin and realize that it is God's kindness that calls you to see yourself for who you are. Romans 2:4 says, "Or do you think lightly of the riches of His kindness and forbearance and patience, not knowing that the kindness of God leads you to repentance?" When people point out our mistakes, we don't often take it as a kindness.

As a writer, I have editors whose pens freely draw my attention to incomplete thoughts and disjointed paragraphs. They are in my life to show me how I can communicate my thoughts more clearly. To do this, they must draw my attention to the faults in my manuscripts. I know there will never be a day that I will write a book, a magazine article, or even a chapter that wouldn't be made better with some editing. Though the pages of revisions may be a heavy burden at first, it is good for me to realize the need for change if I am going to reach my goal of communicating the thoughts I want to share. Likewise, God wants us to open ourselves up to the knowledge of our sins, so that we can become who He longs to help us be. It is only through His strength and power that we can overcome our weaknesses. We don't like this because we want to do it through our own efforts.

As we saw earlier, one of the resistances to receiving God's love is our effort to earn it rather than opening up to God. Too many people have tried to earn God's love because they feel overwhelmed and doomed by guilt. Usually, the guilt they are feeling is not true guilt. God gives us guilt out of His kindness to us. God's guilt is a life-giving, energizing guilt. In 2 Corinthians 7:9–11, Paul compared worldly sorrow (false guilt) and godly sorrow (true guilt). Sorrow that God gives (true guilt) produces repentance without regret; leads to salvation; makes you want to vindicate yourself; gives you indignation for injustice; and develops in you a reverent fear of God and a longing, as well as a zeal, to follow Him more closely. Worldly sorrow (false guilt) produces hopelessness and death.

Diane felt she deserved to be divorced from Tim from the beginning because of a sexual sin she committed just after their marriage.

Vulnerable as a law student and upset with Tim about the pregnancy, she met a professor at his home to work on a project. The professor had other ideas for the evening. Overpowered by her own attraction to the man, Diane let things go too far. She never told Tim. Years later she still thought she was a horrible person, even though she had confessed her sin to God the night it happened.

The remorse she felt was not God's kind, patient guilt. It was the worldly sorrow Paul spoke of in 2 Corinthians 7. God did hold Diane accountable for her vows of faithfulness to her husband. But it wasn't God who had been accusing her of adultery all those years. God forgave her the night she asked His forgiveness. The sin related to this incident that she still needed to confess was her sin of not accepting this forgiveness. Romans 8:1 says, "There is therefore now no condemnation for those who are in Christ Jesus."

When Diane admitted her sin to the women in the group and received their acceptance, she began to believe that God had forgiven and accepted her, too. It gave her even more of an incentive to obey Him. She recognized how sin had messed up her life, and she at last began to believe that God's ways are best after all. She committed herself to following His directions, especially regarding sex and relationships now that she was divorced.

What keeps you from God? Are you letting Satan block you by his constant accusations? Believe that there is no condemnation to those who are in Christ Jesus. Be courageous and open up your heart to Him.

3. Keep Pursuing God

Did you ever think you were lost when you weren't? In Dallas, our baseball team may not always have a winning season, but it does have a first-class stadium. Since I'm more of a fan of the atmosphere than of watching every minute of the game, I often get up to explore the shops and restaurants in the stadium. Once during a game, I decided to take a look at a new store that had opened on the opposite side of the stadium. Before I left, I asked for directions. A courteous usher told me how to get to my destination. As I walked, I began to doubt that I had heard correctly. *Surely I passed the staircase he mentioned. Maybe the double doors he told me to go through were back at that balcony.* But as I pressed onward, I discovered my destination clearly; it was just as he said it would be.

God promises that He will be found. Jeremiah 29:11–14 and 2 Chronicles 7:14 are promises that if we seek Him, He will reveal Himself to us. This does not mean that we will get instant answers or instant relief. It is our consistent desire to see Him for who He is that clarifies our vision of Him. I like the answer God gave the author of the famous "Footprints" poem when she asked Him why she saw His footprints beside her during the easy times of life but not when times were rough. He told her, "That was when I carried you." He gives the same answer to us. We must remember that He is always with us.

Begin pursuing God right now by asking Him to show Himself to you. When I was 15 years old, I was rebellious and running from God. It was at a Christian camp that I first sensed that I was missing out on something. I can't remember any particular person who inspired me through words or example to want to know God. I think I was affected more by the general atmosphere at the camp. I sensed that God was as real as a dear friend and that He wanted the best for my life.

During a few minutes alone in my cabin, I spoke out loud: "God, it seems that some people here know You in an exciting way. I would like to know You that way, too." Then I jumped off my bunk to live my life as I always had. But by slow increments, God began to change me. He had me spend the whole summer away from my friends. I read a Christian book, and the camp counselor gave me a piece of notebook paper with some verses on it to read. I have been reading my Bible daily ever since.

If you seek Him, He will be found.

4. Pray and Listen

In the group, Sharon pondered aloud, "Can knowing God really be as simple as talking and listening to Him?" Then she asked, "How have I been so involved with the church all these years and not been involved with God?"

Regina smiled. "God is a person, right? A divine person, but a person. It takes time to know Him. But basically you get to know God in the same way you get to know ordinary people. You listen to them, learn the things they like and don't like, discover what you have in common, encourage each other, get angry at each other, be there for each other, and before you know it, you have an intimate and lasting relationship."

So easy, yet so difficult. After all, this is God we're talking about. But the principle works.

God used the meeting with Mary Ellen to jostle and dislodge all the pat notions Sharon had about Him. To begin to grasp a vision of who He was, Sharon imagined how He might act if He were living in the twentieth century. As she dodged grumpy drivers during her commute to work, she asked herself, "How would Jesus drive?" She thought about Jesus as she went to church and wondered, "What would Jesus say to this congregation today if He stood up there in that pulpit?" Little by little, God became real and loving to her. Every day He convicted her, inspired her, comforted her, and most of all loved her. She had met a God she couldn't control and was discovering the pure delight of this reality.

Praying and listening to God is really quite simple. Talk to God, read His Word, listen in prayer. Remember that a one-way conversation (you listing all your requests) doesn't promote intimacy. Understand the dynamics of allowing a two-way relationship to develop. Be quiet in God's presence; let Him speak to your heart; let Him lead you to His Word, where He will show you His thoughts and instructions. Time, prayer, and listening will lead you to God so He can guide you on your journey.

Don't expect too much too fast. I like the way Henry Drummond compared what happens in our lives as we spend time with God to what happens in nature:

> Nothing that happens in the world happens by chance. God is a God of order. Everything is arranged upon definite principles and never at random. The world, even the religious world, is governed by law. Character is governed by law. Happiness is governed by law. The Christian experiences are governed by law. Men, forgetting this, expect Rest, Joy, Peace, Faith, to drop into their souls from the air like snow or rain. But in point of fact, they do not do so; and if they did they would no less have their origin in previous activities and be controlled by natural law. Rain and snow do drop from the air, but not without a long previous history. They are the mature effects of former causes. Equally so are Rest, and Peace, and Joy.[3]

Once we start listening to God, we will discover that He has much to say to us about the relationships that tug so deeply at our souls. In fact, He is the only One who can heal us from the damage caused by our relationships. The healing begins through forgiveness. We'll go there next.

CHAPTER TWELVE

Forgiveness: Healing from Damaged Relationships

As we recognize our belovedness, we are still aware of the damaged parts of our souls that are in need of healing. In the arms of the Healer, we are invited to a totally new way of looking at the hurts (rejection from parents, friends, husbands, boyfriends, and children) that have created scars deep in our souls. Rather than trying to control relationships, we are asked to forgive. I hope to help you discover the freedom that forgiveness brings to your wounded places.

For Judy, the word *forgiveness* sent up red flags. She felt that the worst possible decision she could make would be to forgive her father and brother for what they had done to her. She was doing the best she could just to survive in this world. Surviving meant moving 300 miles away from her abusers. To forgive would seem like moving right back into that horrible situation.

Who thought up forgiveness? Walter Wangerin calls forgiveness a "divine absurdity."[1] I like this definition for two reasons. First, the word *absurdity* does fit when you think of forgiving a person who has committed a heinous act against you. In Judy's case, the act was not only against her body but also against her soul. This is always the case in sexual abuse. In fact, usually more damage is done to the soul than to the body. In human terms, it is truly absurd to forgive such an act. Once we get in touch with the rage over what has been done to an innocent child, our natural tendency is to strike back and make the perpetrator pay. Why make such an absurd move as forgiving the person? Because it is divine and because God, the One who loves our souls, asks us to do it.

Before I ever forgave myself or helped others forgive, I always thought forgiveness granted all the benefits to the offender. In the process of struggling with forgiveness, I have found that it is my own soul that receives the greatest benefit from it. I have witnessed amazing changes in people through the healing power of forgiveness. I've seen people become free from panic disorders, suicidal depressions, and bulimia, each by the doorway of forgiveness. Bitterness is replaced by love, joy, and laughter; a life is freed up to enjoy relationships with God and others.

We move off the cycle of damaging relationships when we move toward God and in the direction of forgiveness. We heal the hurts in our relationships with the balm of forgiveness. How does this happen?

In counseling, Judy dug out years and years of anger against her abusers, an emotion she had once turned on herself through depression and attempted suicide. Her Christian counselor encouraged her to face the rage in her soul as a part of the forgiveness process. At first this seemed very "unchristian" to Judy, but through doing it, she understood why it was so necessary to freeing her soul. To help you decipher what Judy learned about forgiveness, let's first consider what forgiveness isn't.

What Forgiveness Isn't

Forgiveness Is Not Going Through the Motions

I have met many men and women in the Christian community who have been instructed to forgive those who have offended them, so they obediently go through the motions. But they have not practiced true forgiveness, in which God also has a part. Instead, they have forgiven in their own ability. The result is nothing more than a Band-Aid on an infected wound. It conceals the wound from others passing by, but allows a fatal infection to grow in the soul. John 6:63 says, "It is the Spirit who gives life; the flesh profits nothing; the words that I have spoken to you are spirit and are life." There is nothing more healing to a damaged soul than forgiveness. It is God through the Spirit who gives us the freedom of true forgiveness. But if you forgive through the flesh—false forgiveness—you will profit nothing.

Forgiveness Is Not Forgetting

You've heard the expression "Forgive and forget." True forgiveness is not forgetting. That is senility. Nowhere in the Bible does it say to "forgive and forget."

I will always remember the most significant experiences of forgiveness in my life. These memories are of spiritual victories, whereby God overcame the fear, rage, and resistance created in my soul by another person's action toward me. In true forgiveness, I release my hatred, self-protection, and desire for vengeance, but I keep all of my short- and long-term memories. When we've experienced the healing power of forgiveness, we can never forget the release we feel in our souls. Through forgiving, we are able to forget "what lies behind" and reach forward to "what lies ahead" (Phil. 3:13), which involves letting go of the pain—being freed from hate, fear, and bitterness.

We remember those painful circumstances in a way that gives us hope for the future. True forgiveness gives us our lives back.

Forgiveness Is Not Denial

Forgiveness is not denying the offense or masking the hurt. That is lying.

It was important for Judy to face her rage in order to find true healing through forgiveness. A part of that included confronting her brother. (Her father had died, so she couldn't confront him this way.) The confrontation would not be a wild outburst. She would be specific about the acts of sexual violation, as well as the vile feelings she carried because of his actions against her.

When Jesus hung on the cross, He died for every sin you and I will ever commit. Second Corinthians 5:21 says He became sin for us. Our Savior didn't smile and say, "Oh, they really aren't that bad." No, He was deeply and completely acquainted with our wretchedness. That was the only way He could forgive us for everything. We can't forgive a transgression if we won't let ourselves face how angry, hurt, and betrayed we were by the offense.

Forgiveness Is Not an Emotion

Forgiveness is not an emotion. We decide to forgive, and we don't automatically feel happy about it. One sign of false forgiveness is instant happiness. I remember watching the aftermath of a well-publicized Christian scandal. A woman related to the scandal was being interviewed on a talk show. During the interview, the woman mentioned one man whom she blamed for everything that went wrong. Near the end of the interview, she was asked what she would do if that man for whom she had such contempt walked out on the stage.

She answered, "Oh, I would probably just walk up to him and hug him and forgive him, because that's the kind of person I am."

At that moment, I realized that she had absolutely no idea of what forgiveness really is. It seemed to me more likely that if that man came into her presence, she might be unwilling to talk about her negative feelings, but that is not forgiveness. Forgiveness is not an action we take without agony of the soul. It is not easy to do. For me, forgiveness begins as a decision to trust God, rather than as a desire or feeling of wanting to be close to the person who has offended me.

Forgiveness Is Not Reconciliation

As Jesus hung on the cross and shed His blood on our behalf, He was willing to forgive the sins of every person that has been or ever will be born. But He certainly has not been reconciled to everyone. He is only reconciled to those who are willing to admit their need for forgiveness. In the same way, reconciliation can only be experienced when offending parties are willing to admit their actions. In Judy's case, forgiving her tormentors and returning to pre-abuse family togetherness are not in the same package.

It is freeing to know that our part of forgiveness doesn't depend on the response of the offender. However, reconciliation does depend on the offender. Reconciliation is only possible when the forgiver and the person being forgiven can come to terms about the offense.

Forgiveness Is Not Being Revictimized

Many victims like Judy resist the idea of forgiveness because they fear it means they will have to place themselves in a trusting position and risk being used again. Forgiveness does not mean being revictimized. True forgiveness cleanses our hearts of the damage caused by an offense. In the process of forgiveness, we realize the need for boundaries—decisions we make about our relationship to the offender that prevent the relationship from being unhealthy, that prevent us from being revictimized. Boundaries are knowing what we are responsible for. In Judy's case, though she forgave her brother, she never put herself in a position to be abused by him again.

Time for You

Who has hurt you most deeply?

Do you feel you have forgiven that person?

Did you recognize yourself in any of the characteristics of false forgiveness?

It is easy to practice false forgiveness, but there is nothing less satisfying to the soul. One day I thought I would save money by buying a different sliced cheese. I didn't realize when I picked it up that it was imitation cheese. It didn't go over too well with the family, so it was a total waste of money. Likewise, we can waste a lot of time, effort, and energy buying into false forgiveness.

Next, we will look at the path of true forgiveness and consider the process of healing the wounds in our souls.

What Forgiveness Is

While jogging at five in the morning, I tripped on an uneven sidewalk and fell flat on my face. I skinned not just my knees, but my hand and shoulder as well. It gave me a whole new compassion for my children when they come to me with their skinned knees. As the scabs were forming, it seemed like forever until I had new, healed skin. One day, though, the skin that once was torn and bruised had turned fresh and pink. Healing wasn't instantaneous or without scars, but it happened. Forgiveness heals the wounds in our souls in much the same way.

What does it mean to truly forgive? How did Judy experience forgiveness in her life? Let's consider the path to true forgiveness.

Forgiveness Is a Process

Forgiveness takes time; it's a process. We don't wake up one day and instantly forgive. We may make the decision to forgive on a certain day, but that just starts the process. For deep offenses, it may take years to experience the full freedom of forgiveness. I compare forgiveness to peeling layers off an onion. You can dig deeply and take off many layers at once, but there are lots of thin layers as well, which makes forgiveness a process of patiently addressing the issues that come up.

Through 10 months of counseling, Judy dug deeply into the layers of unforgiveness encasing her soul. She focused on her relationships with her father, brother, and mother. She grieved over the painful experiences of her childhood. She recognized wrong beliefs she had developed about the world, God, and men from the ways these family members had treated her. But that didn't mean Judy was finished with forgiveness. What began during her counseling would continue throughout her life. The layers would never be as thick as they were at first, but she would remain in the process of forgiving others for as long as she lived.

Forgiveness Is a Decision

Forgiveness isn't a feeling, it is a decision. George MacDonald said, "It may be infinitely less evil to murder a man than to refuse to forgive him. The former may be the act of a moment of passion: the latter is the heart's choice." [2] No one can force us to forgive, and no one can keep us from forgiving. Forgiveness is a decision to trust, not our own instincts, but the voice of God. When I have decided to forgive, it was not because the offender asked me to do this or even acted in a way that created a desire in me to forgive. I forgave because I trusted that God loves me and He would never tell me to do something that wasn't good for me.

Before Judy could make the decision to forgive her brother and deceased father, she had to feel the rage she had hidden within her soul. In the deep recesses of her heart, this rage had turned sour, forming a stubborn, crusty layer of bitterness. The decision to forgive for Judy meant reexamining those tender places. It meant admitting to herself and her counselor that her father and brother had touched her in ways that sealed her sense of being utterly worthless. These were places Judy would rather die than revisit. Yet she found that as she reconsidered them in the context of moving in the direction of forgiveness, they began to lose their power over her.

Her counselor started Judy on the road to forgiveness by asking her to write letters of rage to her brother and deceased father. These were letters she would not send. Rather, they were vehicles by which she let her heart express her legitimate rage and hate against such a horrid assault. Judy did not begin the letters because it felt like a good thing to do. She wrote the letters because she believed that God might show Himself to her through the experience.

We don't have to be fully committed to forgiving someone. It can be a tenuous decision that we make as we trust God to make something happen that is beyond our own control.

Forgiveness Is Desiring Reconciliation

Forgiveness is not reconciliation, but it is desiring reconciliation. One of the litmus tests you can use in your heart to see whether forgiveness has cleansed the wound is to ask yourself if you feel pity or compassion for the one who has offended you.

Notice I said that forgiveness is *desiring* reconciliation, not reconciliation itself. Reconciliation was not possible with Judy's father because he was dead. Nothing about his life indicated to her that he had made peace with God before he died, so she had no assurance that she would see him again. The day she realized she felt hurt for him because he had lived his life causing such harm to others was the day she stopped blaming herself. When forgiveness had healed her soul, she began to see herself as God's beloved daughter and no longer as a victim.

Judy's brother was living, and her mother was also alive. Although her mother had not participated in the sexual abuse, there was a great deal of anger in Judy's heart toward her mother for not protecting her, so it was important for her to examine this relationship as well. Incidentally, Judy's feelings in this regard are natural. A person who has been hurt commonly feels anger toward whomever the victim thinks should have managed a rescue and did not.

What would forgiveness mean to these two relationships? Judy desired to address the issues with her brother more than with her mother, so she began there. She called him and firmly confronted him about the specific ways he had hurt her sexually. She hoped that by confronting him, she might lead him to realize he was accountable for his sinful actions and seek healing himself. She hoped that he might move beyond the sin-drained man he was, toward a new creature in Christ.

God did indeed use Judy's confrontation to move her brother. He began looking at the mess he had made of his life and sought help. Judy learned that her father had abused not only her, but her brother as well. Her brother had reacted to this by abusing Judy for a time and becoming an alcoholic and drug addict. Before Judy's call, God had already been working in his life by bringing him in contact with a Christian ministry in the city where he lived. Judy's step of forgiveness spurred her brother to change.

Judy's mother was a different story. When Judy was ready to contact her mother, she tried to discuss the past over the phone. Her mother simply resorted to her own overpowering, controlling personality and tried to turn the conversation against Judy, insisting that Judy was the problem. Judy was not able to get through to her mother about the forgiveness that was in her heart, so she ended the conversation. She then tried writing to her mother about what she had learned and expressed her desire to have a relationship with her. Judy never received a reply.

Her mother's actions caused more hurt for Judy and more need for forgiveness. Although Judy and her mother were not reconciled, Judy was amazed by the changes that had taken place since she forgave her mom. Instead of never talking to her mother, she called her once a month to chat about safe subjects. When her mother tried to turn the conversation to Judy's endless failures, Judy was able to end the talk. Again, this meant more hurt for Judy, but now she had a remedy as she took her pain and hurt to God and He healed her wounds through forgiveness.

Judy knew that the reconciliation she desired with her mother would never happen unless her mother surrendered her own sinful self-protection and was willing to face the truth about herself. Remember, both parties must desire reconciliation before it will work. Judy was not optimistic that this would happen, but a sprig of hope continued to grow in her soul that it might.

In the meantime, she found herself no longer victimized by her mother but intrigued with the way she could love her. Judy basked in the freedom of knowing that though her mother saw her as a total failure, Judy was no longer a slave to her mother's opinion of her. She saw herself through God's eyes and found that she was able to immediately decipher abusers in relationships, instead of after they had hurt her. Whereas once she saw her life as useless and herself as powerless against those who would victimize her, she now had strong boundaries that kept her healthy and available for God to use her.

Forgiveness Is Alchemy for the Soul

True forgiveness brings about a seemingly magical transformation. Whereas we were once burdened, consumed, and obsessed, now we are transformed, free, and willing. When I was 16 years old, I read a quote that has had a great impact on the way I have lived my life. Here it is: "I will never allow another person to ruin my life by making me hate him."[3] God has used these words to keep my soul free from the burden of hate. Hate creates chemical reactions in our bodies. Unresolved hate and anger have been linked to heart disease and burnout. A soul that is free of hate through forgiveness goes through a chemical transformation.

When the disciples asked Jesus to teach them to pray, one part of the daily prayer He taught was "forgive us our debts, as we also have forgiven our debtors" (Matt. 6:12). Jesus had hard things to say about forgiveness. He said, in essence, "If you do not forgive your brother, how will your heavenly Father forgive you?" (Matt. 6:14–15). Was Jesus teaching that salvation is gained through works? I think Jesus was explaining that forgiveness actually changes our hearts. When we really understand what it meant for Jesus to forgive our sins, we will readily forgive others their sins against us. Our souls are changed from the natural instincts of rage and bitterness into the supernatural instincts of love and forgiveness. Once we have been forgiven, we are not the same.

In the next chapter, we will discuss steps we can take to help us on our journey to forgiveness.

$\mathscr{S}$teps to Forgiveness

I teasingly offer three simple steps to forgiveness when I give a lecture on the subject. I am teasing because these steps are not at all simple. We can narrow it down to a process that involves three phases, but they may take hours or years to complete. This will depend on your heart's condition at the time you begin and the degree of the offense against you. Let's see how Sharon moved through these stages in her journey to forgiveness.

Learning How to Forgive

1. Examine the Full Intensity of the Wrong

Our spirituality won't allow some of us to admit our anger. Convinced that Christians don't get angry, we suffer with souls plagued by unforgiveness, thinking all the while that we are spiritual giants. During the time that Sharon was a leader in her church, this was the state of her heart. She was blistering mad at a husband who took full advantage of her desire to please God by submitting to him. He enjoyed a free ride while Sharon took care of everything. She worked

166 Then God Created Woman

and let him squander the money. He worked only if he felt like it and accepted no responsibility for their daughter. She didn't insist that he go to church or help with housework. Deep inside, Sharon felt that by enduring such a life, her martyrdom would get him saved and then he would immediately become the world's greatest husband. Being a good Christian was her part of the contract to get life to work right. So she was determined not to be angry, because that would not be Christian and might tarnish her image of suffering. But 17 years of this kind of life was all she could handle. When her anger finally surfaced, horrible bitterness poured out. She hated everyone, especially God.

One night Regina led the growth group in an exercise on forgiveness. She had each woman identify one person whom they felt the greatest anger toward. Sharon could say her husband, but her most honest answer was that she was even angrier at God. Regina wasn't shocked by that statement. She encouraged Sharon to begin identifying why she was so angry at Him. In fact, she used that as a lesson for the other women. She told them that in order for them to move beyond the deepest hurts in their lives, they would eventually come against their anger at God. Each of us blames Him (just as Adam did) for allowing us to live in a world that assaults us so deeply.

Each woman wrote a letter expressing her anger. Judy's was addressed to her mother; Joy's, to her husband; Diane's, to her mother; Brenda's, to her father; and Faye's to Rob (who had date-raped her). Sharon, on the other hand, began hers with "Dear God." These letters brought each woman to a place in her heart where she would rather not go.

There are two reasons most of us are afraid to face the intensity of the negative feelings we bear against those who have hurt us. First, we don't want to risk losing those people. Although they have caused us pain, in most cases they have also been important to us.

The second reason we ignore the depth of the offense is that we fear that if we face the way we have been wronged, we may have to accept that we deserved to be treated that way. We retreat from those ugly places in our souls because we fear that they will reveal how ugly we really are.

Well, I've got news for you. We will never experience true forgiveness until we face the rejection clinging to our souls. Earlier in the book, I explained that our souls are not made of Teflon. Rejection sticks, creating a hard coating on our souls. For forgiveness to do its job of cleansing, we must expose this coating. In other words, we have to face how deeply offended we are, even if part of the way our souls have been offended is by anger toward God.

For this reason, Sharon wrote the following:

> Dear God,
> How could You let me marry a man like Ed? You know
> how much love I have to give and what I have to offer.
> I thought You could give us what others seem to get.
> But not me. I am stuck with a man I hate and a daughter
> who is a mess. Maybe I'm not the best mother and that
> is why my daughter is bulimic, but You haven't been
> much of a parent to me either. Why do I have to suffer
> when I've been so good? Why can't You see how hard
> I try?

That night Sharon opened her Bible to Jeremiah 2:13: "For My people have committed two evils: They have forsaken Me, the fountain of living waters, to hew for themselves cisterns, broken cisterns, that can hold no water."

Sharon took a deep breath. At first she felt another lecture coming on. These verses were spelling out two things she had done wrong. Then she thought about her letter. This was God's response to her anger. He was giving her direction; this was not a backlash for attacking Him. She thought of Mary Ellen, and her heart softened. She wanted to hear more than "You're not doing the right thing"; she also wanted to understand exactly what it was that she was doing wrong.

As she meditated, she heard her Father tell her, "You have forsaken Me." Well, that wasn't news. Everyone in church who bothered to ask where Sharon had disappeared to knew that she had forsaken God. But Sharon didn't perceive that statement as a judgment: "You're a bad girl. You have forsaken Me." Rather, for the first time, she sensed that God's heart was deeply grieved by her action. She began to realize that the fact that she had forsaken God really bothered Him and that He wanted her back.

Sharon also recognized, with the Holy Spirit's leading, how she was mistaken about something else. She thought God was the one who had failed her, but Jeremiah 2:13 helped her realize that she was the one who was trying to hold water in a broken cistern—her husband. She had heard Christian women describe loving and spiritual relationships with their husbands, and she had decided that that was the only kind of relationship that could satisfy her soul. She had set out to get it in her own strength. In effect, she had tried to earn it from God. She had read 1 Peter 3:1 as a contract. She figured she had done what she needed to do, but all the time she had been trying to put water in a container that couldn't hold any. The truth of her life was revealed to her as she shattered the hard edges of unforgiveness by examining her anger toward God.

You may write a letter of anger to God and open His Word and not receive the glorious insights Sharon received. Each person is unique and is therefore treated that way by God. His dealings with you will not mirror exactly His dealings with others. I encourage you to share the word, verse, or impression you received with a mature Christian. Let that person be used by the Holy Spirit to reveal God's words to you. Jeremiah 29:13–14 says, "'And you will seek Me and find Me, when you search for Me with all your heart. And I will be found by you,' declares the LORD." Keep seeking. He promises to reveal Himself when you seek Him with all of your heart.

So you don't feel alone in your willingness to face what is in your heart against God, read Joshua 7:6–15 and Psalm 73:21–24. Realize that many great men of God have been angry with Him, too. Even Martin Luther admitted his intense anger toward God as he struggled to know Him more intimately.[1] Our human eyesight often blinds us to God's divine intentions. We blame Him for situations He died to redeem.

At the same time that it is difficult to acknowledge our anger toward God, it is also difficult to acknowledge our anger toward those who have offended us. But true forgiveness will never come until you have the courage to do this.

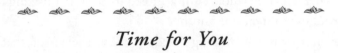

Time for You

Write a letter expressing your anger toward the person you identified in the preceding chapter as someone you need to forgive.

2. Take Responsibility for Your Own Sins

After Sharon finished listing the many offenses she had attributed to God, she was amazed by His patient response to her. Then she began to see her own responsibility for the state of her life. Perhaps her trying to do it all had driven her husband and daughter away from her. She had expected so much of them because she had expected so much of herself. She no longer blamed God for her husband's refusal to accept Him as Savior. She knew that God created him with a free will and that no one wanted him to come to God through Christ more than God Himself did. She saw how trying to control God had prevented her from forming deep and meaningful relationships. She had been focused on being good for God so He would make her husband and daughter the people she wanted them to be. Now she saw how controlling she had been with them. Even moving out had been a control move. Totally frustrated because her old methods hadn't worked, she had tried a new one. This one may have gotten more attention, but it only served to accentuate the problems.

Sharon felt convicted to have a talk with her husband and daughter. She told her husband that she had been wrong to leave and that she was willing to come back if he wanted to work on the marriage. She told her daughter that she was sorry for having had unrealistic expectations of her and for the fact that they were destroying her. The whole family agreed to go to counseling to try to learn how to treat one another.

Sharon was finally finding freedom from the anger that had consumed her. She stopped blaming God and took responsibility for herself. This has made all the difference. Her countenance has changed so dramatically that people at work keep asking her if she has had a face-lift. All of this is the result of releasing anger through forgiveness.

Time for You

Identify the damage you have done to yourself by hanging on to anger.

3. **Commit to a Heart of Forgiveness Through God's Strength**

Sharon and Ed's relationship didn't improve instantly just because Sharon came home. But Sharon was determined to change, and some of the changes had to be in the amount of work she did around the house. She realized it was wrong of her not to hold Ed accountable as a husband. Symbolic of all this was the stack of dishes in the sink.

In her household, dishes piled up in a hurry, and somehow Sharon always ended up washing them. Her daughter had drama practice, homework, or some other activity; and Ed had his channel surfing. In counseling, Ed promised to help with some of the work around the house, and dishes were a part of the deal. This meant that Sharon must leave the dirty dishes in the sink if Ed failed to do them. Each time Ed neglected to live up to a promise he had made in a counseling session, Sharon had new opportunities to forgive. It was a tough road and definitely not a case of happily-ever-after, but at least Sharon found she had a choice in addressing her feelings. Instead of doing the dishes so that God would change her husband, she didn't do them and asked God to help her respectfully talk to Ed about the disappointments in their marriage.

The Freedom of True Forgiveness

True forgiveness is one of the most important instructions Jesus gives us. The reality of a fallen world makes forgiveness the only true remedy to the damage done to our souls by hurtful relationships. I challenge you to consider the deep work of forgiveness and let God know that you are willing to practice true forgiveness in your relationships. As you practice true forgiveness, you are well on your way toward ending your cycle of damaging relationships. You are ready to go to the third stepping-stone: giving God control.

CHAPTER FOURTEEN

When Control Is Out of Control

Our natural sinful instincts lead us to use control as a way of solving our relationship pain. A friend told me about this incident. She was walking through her neighborhood when a friend's Labrador retriever, Greta, came running across the street to greet her. Greta failed to notice traffic, and a minivan bowled her over to the curb. Slobbering, poor Greta thrashed in the dry leaves of the gutter. My friend and Greta were good buddies and had been for years. But Greta, dazed and frightened, felt threatened. When my friend approached, eager to help, Greta turned on her and ripped her hand. The dog's instincts led her to attack in order to protect herself. My friend backed away and found Greta's owner. Together, they were able to comfort the dog and get her to the vet, where she made a complete recovery.

Greta's instincts were to bite in order to ward off more pain. Human beings are like that, too. Our instincts to attack and control in order to protect ourselves greatly complicate our relationships because control has a way of turning on us. At first it offers comfort because we don't feel as vulnerable. But after a while, control becomes a compulsion. By that time, we are not even aware that we are making a choice. This is how control destroys our lives. When we, like Greta, lie in the gutter, overwhelmed by our pain, our attempts to control our pain keep us from receiving what we need most.

Let's begin by looking at a personal control scale and discover how tightly the control cycle grips our lives. How controlling are you? Is your control style obvious, or do you use the victim mode? Consider the following questions to evaluate your own control intensity. Place a check by any statements that are true of you.

Personal Control Scale

_____ I know that the best place for my children (or those I love most) is in God's hands.

_____ I am a forgiving person.

_____ People aren't always complaining that I have to be in charge.

_____ My closest friends (or children) do not think I try to run their lives.

_____ It's OK for me not to know what I am going to do tomorrow.

_____ I enjoy unstructured free time at least once a week.

_____ I could honestly tell God that I'm willing to go anywhere to serve Him, if that is His desire.

_____ If I feel the Holy Spirit prodding me to speak to someone about Christ, I do so, even though I might feel embarrassed.

_____ I don't end up doing the majority of work on the committees I serve on.

_____ At least one other person knows the most painful events of my life and has been supportive.

_____ I don't try to look all together on the outside and hide my real vulnerability.

_____ I don't mind admitting my weaknesses.

_____ Vulnerability isn't a scary thought for me.

_____ I know I'm vulnerable to God, and I wouldn't have it any other way.

_____ I know of at least five areas of my life that all the effort in the world would not give me control over.

_____ I don't feel used by others when I reach out to them and they don't respond.

_____ When working on group projects, I don't feel I have to take over or do everything myself.

_____ When someone tells me a problem, I just listen. I don't feel I have to provide the right answer.

_____ I don't feel overwhelmed with responsibilities.

_____ I rarely have critical thoughts about others.

Total checks ✕ 5 = _____

Control Scale Results

95–100—*Saint.* You are so perfectly at peace with God and yourself that you have no control issues. Or you weren't completely honest with yourself when you took this test.

85–95—*Flexible.* You have discovered that control doesn't solve your problems. You yield yourself to God and others.

75–85—*Bending.* You are aware of a desire for control and battle within yourself between controlling people and situations and yielding these to God.

65–75—*Control-Minded.* You are caught in a life of control and are in bondage trying to control others.

55–65—*Rigid.* You have a controlling outlook and find it difficult to see that control is an illusion.

45–55—*Controlling Personality.* You are deceived by control and are committed to making life work your way.

45 and under—*Control Freak.* You are living to control people, events, and circumstances and believe control is mandatory for existence.

Why We Control

In counseling I have a rule of thumb: The more controlling the person, the more shame, anger, and fear he or she is hiding. When you first meet someone like Sharon, you might think she has a lot of anger, but you wouldn't consider shame or fear. In fact, she was pretty fearless to confess her feelings of anger toward God in the growth group. But Sharon possessed a great deal of fear and shame that she hid from herself as well as from others. The more controlling you are, the more you need to explore your fear, anger, and shame. Let's look at how these three feelings—that every one of us experience—lead to the desire to be in control.

Fear

In his book *Powerful Personalities,* Tim Kimmel wrote: "Fear makes us think our problems can be solved if we just hold on a little tighter to the things and people we love the most."[1] Sharon would say that the responsibilities she had as the oldest daughter of six children helped her become a trustworthy and capable woman. But what she wouldn't let herself consider was why she had so much responsibility, at what age she was first given this responsibility, and whether her life had been negatively affected by feeling so responsible.

Sharon can remember being six years old and her mother dragging her out of bed and instructing her to be a good girl and take care of anything the babies might need. This would happen around 10:00 P.M. when her mother had the urge to go to a bar and have some fun. She wouldn't come back until around 3:00 or 4:00 A.M. She would always praise Sharon for being such a big help and tell her that she needed that time because all those babies drove her crazy. Sharon was always willing to do this because the alternative, having her mom go crazy, was worse than the terror she felt being responsible for the household at night while her mom was gone.

After her mother would leave, Sharon would crawl up on the couch, look out into the darkness, and cry for her mommy, the normal response of a young child in that position. There she would stay until her mother returned. Her mother seemed to think she could do the job, so Sharon thought something was wrong with her for being so afraid to be home alone and baby-sitting at six. Fear of being responsible for something too big for her created the insatiable need for control in Sharon's life. Sharon's fear that she wasn't big enough drove her to never show that responsibility frightened her.

People at work thought of Sharon as a successful person. When she was involved in church, she was always welcome to lead others. At work and church and in the community, her controlling personality was rewarded time after time. Sharon's control met its match in her relationship with her daughter, Linda. Linda was 17 and bulimic.

Linda grew up believing that Sharon was perfect. It seemed Sharon always made the right decisions, and Linda felt she just couldn't live up to the pressure of a perfect mom. She found that eating and purging accomplished many things for her: She could control one area of her life that her mother couldn't, she could stay thin to please her mother, and she could prove that she was a failure because she couldn't even eat right.

If Sharon would face her fears of doing something wrong, she could be a better mother by showing Linda how to make and recover from mistakes, rather than imposing impossible standards on her.

Anger

Anger is obvious in people like Sharon, Diane, and Brenda, but not so detectable in people like Judy, Joy, and Faye. Don't let that deceive you. Those are the ones who need to look at their anger the most. In fact, every time someone called Faye to ask her to bake some more cookies or join a new committee, Faye felt angry. She was so afraid of admitting anger that she would simply smile, all the while hating herself and the person who was asking this new task of her. Faye had never learned how to resolve her anger. She tried to control it with sweetness. What she needed to do was acknowledge that she was angry and choose how to express it. Sometimes the anger was a sign that she was overcommitted and needed to say no.

Faye had good reason to feel rage about the boy who date-raped her in high school. She had buried that rage in the same place she put all of her anger through the years. The reason she rebelled against her parents was her anger at them. She would never have expressed it directly, so she rebelled indirectly. Nothing for Faye was open and honest, since she was so diligent in repressing her "bad" emotions. This disguised all of her feelings and prevented her from making decisions about what she wanted to do and why she might not be right for a certain committee or task. Because she repressed her negative emotions, she became confused about whether something was right for her to do. Emotions can give us insights into ourselves. Not feeling negative emotions such as anger left Faye confused and outwardly sweet, but inwardly unhappy. In her effort to control her anger, she got out of control in volunteering. This led to a sense of being even more out of control when her family got angry with her for not being available for them.

When Faye accepted her anger and tuned in to what she might have been angry about, she was better able to make decisions. Recently, someone from her daughter's school called to ask if she could fill in at the last minute and organize the school's international festival. The woman who had volunteered was having personal problems and couldn't do it. The festival was only one week away, and the woman had done nothing to prepare. The caller went on to remind Faye of the wonderful job she had done organizing the school's spring roundup and told her that she was practically the only woman who could do a job like this. Faye said she would think about it and get right back to her. The moment she hung up the phone, the impossibility of the task hit her.

I know I did a great job with the roundup, she thought, *but that was because I had months to plan, call, and prepare.*

She considered all the last-minute calling and imposing she would have to do to organize the festival. She realized that if she felt pressured and irritated, the other volunteers might feel the same way. Faye called the woman back and explained that, in her opinion, the school should postpone the international festival because there was no way it could be done adequately in that little time. The woman seemed cool and disappointed in Faye for saying no. It wasn't easy for Faye to do, but she knew it was the best decision. A few months later, the international festival went off without a hitch, and Faye was happy to help in a smaller way.

Shame

Shame is the greatest source of our need to control. Everyone has shame, but there is legitimate and illegitimate shame.

Illegitimate shame is a pervasive sense of worthlessness. It is accompanied by a sense of isolation and fear that if I am truly known, I will be rejected or abandoned. Judy's illegitimate shame stemmed from the sexual abuse she had suffered. She accepted the shame and believed that something was wrong with her or men wouldn't treat her the way they did. Illegitimate shame is different from legitimate shame.

Legitimate shame is God-given and is the result of sinning against Him. It shows us our inability to make life work on our own. Its antidote is relationship with Jesus Christ. Diane felt legitimate shame that night she confessed her sin of adultery. But later she was suffering from illegitimate shame, along with false guilt, when she believed, "Once an adulteress, always an adulteress."

Shame, whether legitimate or illegitimate, is such a negative emotion that we want to get away from it as soon as possible. We turn to control, hoping we will find some kind of immunity. But the only healing from shame comes as we face it before God and let Him reveal to us whether it is legitimate or illegitimate. If it is legitimate, we need to confess our sin, and God will forgive us. If it is illegitimate, we need to see who the shame really belongs to and give it back to them.

The effects of fear, anger, and shame lead us in the direction of controlling others. But most of us don't stop there. We even try to control God.

Why We Try to Control God

It's so easy to approach God looking for formulas to make life work, instead of for a relationship. I find myself identifying with Sharon, wanting to read a Bible verse and demand that God give me what I want because I have obeyed a scripture. Just as we resist God's love, we also try to control Him.

One reason we try to control God is that we are more interested in getting from Him than being with Him. We want safety or insurance. We try to control God because although we want a Supreme Being, an eternal Father, who will right all the wrongs in the world, we don't necessarily want someone suggesting the best way for us to live.

A second reason we try to control God is that we don't want to take any risks with our lives. We want things to turn out the way we plan them. As a teenager I was afraid to commit my future to God lest He would make me be a single missionary nurse in Africa. At 17 years old, I couldn't think of anything worse than that. Then after much prayer and soul-searching, I finally surrendered and told God that I was willing to do whatever He wanted me to do. Come to find out, He didn't want me to be a missionary nurse in Africa at all. Today I'm a happily married Christian counselor living in the United States. God really does know best.

A third reason we try to control God is our fear of being exposed as inadequate or out of step. Letting the Holy Spirit guide and lead us isn't exactly going with the flow of the world. One time God led me to begin a prayer group. He gave me the names of several female friends to invite. Reluctantly, I obeyed His prompting. I sent them postcards inviting them to come to my house for a "community of prayer." I didn't know how they would respond to the invitation or even if they would come. They all did come, and now we have a special bond because of the prayers we have prayed for one another. I treasure their support as I speak, do radio interviews, and write. If I had gotten stuck worrying about whether they thought I was strange, I would have missed out on this significant part of my life. God longs for us to focus on Him, not on what people might think of us.

These three reasons we try to control God are all rooted in our deep fear of being out of control. In my journey to know God, I have sought formulas, but God never gives them to me. He gives me direction—a little hint here, a big insight there—but He always remains God. He doesn't let me control Him. And in the end, I wouldn't have it any other way.

When Control Becomes Compulsion

What controlling people often don't realize is how out of control they can become. For example, controllers often become compulsive. A compulsion develops when a behavior, such as eating or gambling, starts controlling you.

Joy was compulsive in her spending habits. That was one of the reasons she worked at the dress shop—so she could get a discount on clothes. Joy's husband was successful financially, but he sensed that Joy's spending was out of control because she could never stay on a clothing budget. One week he totaled her expenses and found that she had gone to the mall every day and had spent several thousand dollars on clothing and accessories for herself and their daughters. At this point he insisted that she could spend only the cash he gave her each week, in addition to the money she made at her job. It was a generous amount, but it was never enough for Joy.

Joy didn't realize that no amount of money would ever be enough because she was seeking to feel good through her extravagant spending. Joy liked owning beautiful things and wearing beautiful clothes, because these things meant she would get attention for being attractive. Joy clung to beauty for a sense of identity.

Because Joy was so desperate for her husband's approval and because she felt bad for having so many material blessings, she conceded and limited her compulsive spending to the amount of money her husband budgeted. But because she had not yet addressed her false sense of identity fueling her compulsion (she had only tamed it by sticking to the agreement she made with her husband), Joy soon began another compulsion: She started reading romance novels and renting and watching romance movies.

This second compulsion became so extreme that Joy would miss out on activities with her family and friends because she was in the middle of a new book or wanted to watch a movie. Many of us are consumed by a movie or book from time to time, but Joy's habit was getting out of control. This compulsion was driven by the same emptiness that led to her "shop-aholic" tendencies. It gave Joy a sense of being loved. She would put herself in the place of the heroine and dream that she was the love interest the hero could not live without. These fantasies helped her escape from the nagging fear that anyone who really knew her would be disgusted.

Her compulsion created tension in her family. Her husband and daughters became increasingly irritated that she could become so focused on a book or movie that she forgot about them.

The Illusion of Control

I was pregnant with Benjamin, my second child, when my husband and I received a call from Focus on the Family inviting us to do an interview for our new book, *Passages of Marriage.* This was quite an honor, and I was really happy that Brian—along with our coauthors, the Minirths and Hemfelts—would be able to represent us. Brian wanted me to go, but I thought that was absurd. After all, I was nine months pregnant and three feet high—lying down! I agreed to call my doctor and ask his opinion, certain that he would say, "Absolutely not."

To my surprise, he said, "Well, the medical care in Colorado Springs is just as good as it is in Dallas. It really has to be your decision."

I told Brian I would pray about it. He said that he couldn't say for sure that God was telling him I should go, but he insisted that I consider the trip. So I called the airline. The date we were to go to Colorado Springs was 10 days before my due date, and the airline said that I could fly up to seven days before that date with no restrictions.

My mother was scheduled to fly in the day before we were to go for the interview. Her plane reservations had been made several months in advance. I knew I could count on her to say, "I can't be a part of this."

But she said, "Well, if you decide to go, isn't it great that I'll already be there to baby-sit Rachel?"

I kept reading the Bible and asking God to give me a verse saying that I should stay so I could show it to Brian. One of the passages I turned to was Psalm 139 because I knew that in it David spoke about himself in the womb. Verse 5 stood out for me: "Thou hast enclosed me behind and before, and laid Thy hand upon me." All the scriptures I read expressed the same thought to me: *What makes you think you are so safe if you stay in Dallas? I am the One who keeps you safe no matter where you are.*

The morning of the flight, I reluctantly decided to go. I packed a bag even though we were only going for the day. I also packed an outfit for the baby and things I might need in a hospital. We went to the airport, and I waddled aboard the plane, still uncertain that I was doing the right thing. I kept telling Brian that I wanted God to give me a sign.

About halfway through the flight, I got up to use the rest room, something pregnant women do a lot.

A woman leaned over the seat and said to Brian, "Sir, do you mind me asking how far along your wife is?"

"Ten days before her due date."

The woman smiled. "Do you realize that you are on a plane with 21 gynecologists who are on their way to Colorado Springs for a conference?"

When I got back, Brian crowed, "I've discovered your sign from God!"

"My sign from God will be when I set my feet back down in Dallas with the baby still inside me."

And that is just what happened. In fact, Benjamin was born exactly seven days later, happy and healthy.

There's nothing that has helped me grow in love and intimacy with God more than giving Him my fears and anxieties. At the same time, there is nothing more frightening, frustrating, and foreign to me than letting go. We are all controllers, some more aggressive than others.

Women continually tell me that it is hard for them to give their children, careers, spouses, or finances completely to God. They fear that giving them to God would be dangerous. They are functioning on a significant lapse of logic. It is the illusion of control. What control do we really have in this world anyway? Even a strongly controlling person like Sharon felt disappointed with her life. Believe me, if control could get you what you want, Sharon would have been a happy woman. Instead she was haunted by her inability to make life work. Control is an illusion we create to make ourselves more comfortable in this world. How do we overcome this need to control?

Overcoming Our Need to Control

Go to God for Help

We need to see God as the answer to all that our human nature tells us control will give us. Just like the prodigal son, we usually aren't ready to do this until we hit bottom. We have a choice to make. We can either keep trying to control by finding our own way or we can come home to the Father.

Sharon made that choice after she discovered her daughter, Linda, pale and unconscious on the bathroom floor. After Sharon rushed her to the hospital and received the diagnosis of bulimia, reality slammed her between the eyes. Sharon could not force her daughter to have the perfect home life she herself longed for. The meager benefits of control—the fantasy that her daughter was not affected by her own horrible marriage—were soured by the consequences of grasping that she had a very sick child on her hands. Sharon had bottomed out. As she sat dazed in the waiting room, she turned her heart toward God. She confessed that Linda's life was a mess and there was nothing that she as her mom could do about it. She asked God to help Linda get well, physically and emotionally.

The doctor did have some good news. "From what we can tell, Linda's body functions are still normal. But that doesn't mean there are no problems. Her potassium and blood sugar levels, for instance, are very low. Also, I strongly recommend a treatment program, beginning immediately. My office can set it up for you. And now, I believe Linda is waiting for you." His pager beeped, and he hastened away.

When she entered Linda's room, Sharon nearly fainted. She

hadn't realized how emaciated her daughter was. A pallid stick figure lay on the bed, her arm not much bigger than the intravenous tube inserted into it.

A day ago, Sharon would have instantly begun her diatribe, berating Linda, telling her what she should do, informing her of the treatment program she must attend.

That was a day ago.

"I'm sorry, Mom." Linda's voice sounded as feeble as her body looked.

But Sharon was too busy scooping her child into her arms. Through her sobs, she said, "Oh, darling, I'm so, so sorry!"

A gallon of tears later, they began to talk. For the first time ever, they talked person to person, heart to heart. They even laughed together.

Sharon admitted that her excessive control was ruining them both. The growth group had helped Sharon realize that she not only pushed herself to be perfect, but she also pushed Linda—to excel in school and sports, to look good, to live up to the role of the perfect daughter in the perfect family.

Linda confessed that her bulimia was controlling her and she was scared.

Sharon nodded. "I hear you. Do you know how hard it was for me to come in here and tell you I love you instead of starting right into you?"

Linda grinned. "Yeah, I knew something was different."

To Sharon's surprise, over the next few weeks, Linda was amazingly open to hearing what her mother had to say. Both faced a long road ahead, but Sharon at last felt she had a powerful resource—her renewed relationship with Jesus. Though it wasn't easy, Sharon began to rely on God's strength to overcome her natural tendencies to lecture, pressure, and manipulate her daughter.

Admit You Are Powerless

When Joy learned that her favorite miniseries was being repeated, she found herself tense and fearful that she would miss it. That was when she realized she had a big problem. She had transferred her compulsive spending habit to an addiction to romance. Joy decided to go "cold turkey" and made other plans for the four nights the miniseries would be aired. It was tough. When she got home early one night, she couldn't stop herself from watching the last hour of the episode.

When it was over, Joy fell onto her knees and wept. She finally accepted that she was powerless to control her addictions. She told God that she couldn't believe how pathetic her life had become; she felt so empty inside that she couldn't stop herself from watching a television program or buying a new outfit. She asked God to help her see why she had become so compulsive and heal the damaged parts of herself. At that moment, Joy's healing began.

Once you reach the point of admitting you are powerless to make the right choice consistently and productively, you have made the first step in your healing process. The second step is recognizing who *is* powerful!

No one is into power structures more than military regimes, and in Jesus' day, the Roman military machine was the most powerful in the world. There was one Roman officer who truly understood the power of Jesus. If Jesus said He was the Son of God, then He indeed had the power of God. So when this military official's favorite servant lay near death, he sent for Jesus. But he didn't exercise his own power, demanding that Jesus come to him. He knew how Jews felt about entering the home of a Gentile. Yet he considered Jesus powerful enough to just say the word and it would be done. If you read the story in Luke 7:1–10, you will find that it *was* done. Even more amazing were the words Jesus used to describe this man. He told the crowd that this Gentile showed more faith than anyone in Israel. Not even the disciples had that much faith in Jesus.

What power we miss out on to overcome the sins in our lives when we refuse to admit we can't do it on our own! It's like spending the whole afternoon vacuuming the carpet with an unplugged vacuum cleaner. You must plug into the power source or you will never overcome your sin. It is our powerlessness that helps us plug into God's powerfulness. We are the plug, and He is the socket.

When will we believe in the power of Jesus? When will we surrender and admit we are powerless? When we do, we will be on our way to giving God control.

Let Go and Let God

Joy and Sharon had major areas to release to God, and it was helpful for both of them to understand how control had gotten such a strong grip on their lives. It was equally important for them to view God as the One whom they could trust to take care of things.

Joy worked on acknowledging her fear that she wasn't important to anyone apart from what she could do for him or her. As she grew to realize how special and valuable she was to God, she had less need to buy compulsively and she was able to control her addiction to romances.

Sharon, too, grappled with her fears. She confessed that the demands of life were greater than her ability to respond to them and was surprised when she sensed that God had known that all along. She learned that her six-year-old fears (of being in charge of her younger siblings late at night when her mother went out) were warranted. The world is a frightening place, and Sharon learned that she shouldn't be expected to shoulder the burden alone. It was freeing for Sharon to realize why she took so much responsibility for issues she couldn't control. The freedom came in realizing these were issues she would never be able to control. When it came to Linda, all Sharon could do was pray and be there when she needed her—which was what Linda had needed all along. Sharon began to realize the benefits of giving God control.

Letting go happens in big and small ways. When the women's growth group was examining this issue, Regina confessed a struggle she was having. Her daughter had tried out for the school play, and another girl was chosen. The girl who was chosen was the daughter of the director's best friend, and Regina and her daughter suspected that the choice was a biased one. What do you do in that situation? Do you complain to the principal, or do you take it up with the director? How do you decide? What does it mean to let go and let God?

The women had a good discussion about Regina's dilemma and their own. In the end, each was challenged to let go in a particular way. Judy was encouraged to accept a date with a good friend at church. Sharon was asked to confess her 10 worst failures to her daughter. The group challenged Joy to go one whole day without makeup. Diane committed to playing with her children, without an agenda, every night. Brenda was asked to be vulnerable with a new man at work, and Faye agreed to say no to all new commitments. Regina decided to grieve with her daughter about the situation at school and to encourage her to do her best to learn the lesser role.

Wonderful Things Happen When We Give God Control

What can happen when women give God control? Heaven only knows. That's the beauty of it. When we stop striving, we begin to be still. It is only then that we experience God in a deeper way. We can't get anywhere in our relationship with God until we dump our tendency to control. That's why in Jesus' day, though many religious leaders saw Him face to face, they didn't recognize the Person to whom they were speaking. They were too busy controlling God by their religious endeavors to recognize Him when He stood right in front of them.

In the case of the women in the growth group, when they gave God control, some exciting things did happen. At the cast party, a special award was presented to Regina's daughter for having the best team spirit. Judy built up her faith in men by allowing herself to be befriended by a man who didn't try to hurt her. Sharon and Linda developed an imperfect but much improved relationship. Joy was amazed that she would let the pool guy and gardener see her without makeup. Although she didn't go out in public, she was dumbfounded to realize that these two men were as chatty as usual. Diane had a blast with her kids—she discovered that letting them be in charge was fun. Brenda was asked out on a date for the first time in two years. Faye spent an entire evening watching her favorite movie and couldn't stop talking about how much she enjoyed it.

Sooner or later, if you are going to grow in the Christian life, you are going to have to give God control. And I can guarantee that once you do it, you'll never regret it. If only letting go weren't so hard.

CHAPTER FIFTEEN

Practicing Spirituality

Have you ever had one of those burning-earlobe days? One of the ways I recognize that I have reached my stress limit is when my earlobes start burning from the weight of my earrings and I am still out there working. This happens on a night I work late and haven't had a free morning to relax and prepare, or on an evening I have a speaking engagement or some other social event after a full day. My earlobes hurt, my neck muscles tense up, and my eyes burn. It's really bad when I realize that I haven't even had time to go to the bathroom.

Let's face it: We are all too busy. Just as there are more nice things to buy than we have money for, there is much more to do than we have time and energy for. Our souls are craving to hear us say, "Enough." They need time for rest and reflection. They were made that way. The Old Testament principle of Sabbath rest was a gift from our Creator, not a religious regulation.

Women need rest more than men. My husband is amazed by my motto "When I have a long list of things to do, I make sure I mark off my nap first." But I challenged him to try accomplishing things my way for a week, and he discovered it does have its benefits. For instance, he would come home after a hard day at work and always leave his tie on. I finally persuaded him to change into something more comfortable after work so he could relax. It didn't take him long to realize it was much better to return phone calls and do other tasks in comfortable attire. I have been known to put my pajamas on at 6:30 P.M. (I hate to wear my work clothes, but I don't want to do extra laundry either.)

You will never find stillness unless you look for it. And you will never find God unless you make room in your life for stillness. For women to discover the healing power of stillness, they first must recognize why they are so busy. We need to understand our "Type E: Everything to Everybody" syndrome.

Observances of Women

Psychologist Dr. Harriet Braiker offered a fitting definition of women. Through her research observing how stress affects women, she discovered some major differences in how the sexes respond. Although the typical Type A personality—aggressive, competitive, driven—in men correlated to an increase in heart attacks and stress-related illnesses, Braiker found that women who suffered from stress symptoms did not fit the typical Type A profile. Instead, she found stressed-out women were better labeled Type E. She defined the Type E woman as "a woman who thought she had to be everything to everybody."[1] What a fitting definition of women! If we had a chance to get inside the heads of our seven women from the growth group, I bet we would discover that all these women are struggling with inner voices calling them to try to meet the needs and expectations of just about everyone with whom they have a significant relationship. Being a woman and being sensitive to other people's needs seem to go hand-in-hand.

Voices Calling to Us

Because of the way we women are wired, we cannot easily ignore the cries of a child or the needs of an aging mother. We are uniquely attuned to the needs of the people around us. Why is it that a son cannot come home for Christmas and never sheds a tear, while a daughter weeps her eyes out? We have a sixth sense about the emotional state of the people around us. Do you hear voices calling you to meet needs? I struggle daily trying to decipher the voices in my head. Can you relate to this example from my journal?

> I feel guilty for the opportunity to be in my pajamas at 9:00 A.M. Although I have much to do and much that could have kept me busy until now, I have chosen to follow Jesus. I have spent my morning preparing to teach my Sunday class about Luke. I probably wouldn't have planned my day this way, I have so many voices offering their "shoulds."
>
> My Brian voice says, "You should be doing, no time for sitting or reflecting; do laundry, scrub floors, teach Benjamin, go to the grocery store, clean, cook, do, do, do."
>
> My Benjamin voice says, "You should be teaching; I should be able to write my name, recognize the alphabet, numbers, shapes, and colors. I should not be watching TV. I should be having friends over to play with. I should not be so strong-willed. All of this is your fault."
>
> My Debi voice says, "You should have the chapters of your book written and sent off; you should do all those things on Brian's list."
>
> Just now I'm not in touch with the voices that demand still more of me: my Rachel voice, church voice, patients' voices, neighborhood voices. . . . They can go on and on.

Research shows that the differences between men's and women's brains are dramatic. Anne Moir and David Jessel said this about the functioning of women's brains: "A woman is more sensitive than a man in her very being. She is more alert to touch, smell and sound. She sees more and remembers, in detail, more of what she sees. The bias of her brain leads her to attach much more importance to the personal, and interpersonal, aspects of life. Ever since that early eye contact, at a few hours old, she has been more interested in people." [2]

Our tendency to be more sensitive to others and their needs is real and distinguishes us from men. I remember asking my husband to get one-year-old Benjamin out of the high chair. Benjamin had a way of making dinner look like the aftermath of a national disaster. Brian got up from the table, fetched a washcloth, and started cleaning up the mess on the floor while Benjamin, strapped in the high chair, screamed for his release. When I clean up around the high chair, I go for the baby first, then the rest of the mess. Brian easily ignored his son's cries because his mind was set on the task of cleaning up. Women aren't like that. We are extremely sensitive to the people in our lives, and this heightens our franticness.

Time for You

What voices do you hear? Write the names of the voices in your head and the messages they send to you.

Frantic Christianity

The voices we hear, our drive to be everything to everyone, spills into our Christian experiences. Women are particularly susceptible to becoming frantic Christians. I often observe a swirl of frantic Christianity among women in the church. There is plenty to do, and we are just the women to do it. When invited to speak at women's retreats in various parts of the country, I am saddened if I meet women who have given hours of time and effort to a project or program yet can't enjoy the result because their franticness keeps them from receiving what is being offered. I'm not being critical because I know for a fact that it does require a lot of planning, work, and time to create a weekend for women to focus on God. It's just that some women are so focused on the theme that the time to stop and reflect and be touched by God gets crowded out. If God gets crowded out, you have the first clue that you may be practicing frantic Christianity. Frantic Christianity can be defined as being so focused on the tasks of living the Christian life that you miss out on the experience of being with God.

When I am doing what God calls me to do, I am amazed at the ways He takes care of the details. I remember working on a mother-daughter tea and running into someone at the copy machine who was holding the perfect graphics for our event. Little things that I didn't even have time to pray about are taken care of by the God who cares. He even cares about those small things (such as an inexpensive party favor) that seem unnecessary but mean lot to women. God knows that we women like these special touches, and He provides them.

Franticness Comes from the Mirrors We Look Into

Franticness comes from the world's mirrors as they constantly bombard us with ideas of how to better belong here. It comes from the natural instincts of our sinful nature. We strive to be the best, to have it all, to conquer. Without God as the center of our quests, we will find ourselves lost and spinning, chasing the wind and ending up empty. You don't know God by striving, possessing, or conquering.

Romans 11:33 says, "Oh, the depth of the riches both of the wisdom and knowledge of God! How unsearchable are His judgments and unfathomable His ways!" And Job 11:7–8: "Can you discover the depths of God? Can you discover the limits of the Almighty? It is high as the heavens, what can you do? Deeper than Sheol, what can you know?" There is a depth, a height, an awesome reality, a new frontier to discover. But we'll have to throw away the mirrors we look into and learn instead how to become mirrors ourselves—mirrors that reflect the magnificence of our Creator.

Henry Drummond explained, "Christ is the one great fixed point in this shifting universe. But the world moves. And each day, each hour, demands a further motion and readjustment for the soul. . . . The soul passively reflects the image of the Lord, while the will actively holds the mirror in position."[3]

When we reflect on God, the center of the universe, we increasingly take on His likeness, His image. It is an image of peace without a trace of franticness.

Franticness Comes from Our Need to Be Good Enough

Women are so eager to win approval that we will go to extremes to make ourselves liked and accepted. We will busy ourselves trying to excel at work and at home. All the time, we feel a need to be this way without complaining and always with a smile.

Unfranticness is realized when we accept that Jesus made us good enough when we trusted Him to save us. When Regina went to her 20-year college reunion, she became reacquainted with several of her closest friends. Her roommate, Carol, was a judge, and their suitemate JoAnn had been on *Oprah* discussing her latest book. Regina was shocked at her response to her friends' successes. She was genuinely happy for them and genuinely sorry at the same time.

She didn't feel inferior because she was at home raising her three children. In fact, she showed off their pictures as if they were Pulitzer prizes. She could tell by her friends' faces that they couldn't appreciate how special her life was. Yet she didn't feel insulted or envious. Somehow the acclaim of the world had lost its appeal for Regina; she no longer craved its applause.

The opposite of frantic Christianity is patient Christianity. Women are so relationship centered and sensitive to other people's needs that we won't naturally choose the course of patient Christianity. Yet without learning to listen, to be patient in our relationship with God, we will never get to know Him.

Patient Christianity

Patient Christianity involves being still enough and defenseless enough to look into the mirror of your soul and listen as God speaks to you and is with you. It happens when you set aside your business, "Christian work," and all of your excuses. It means looking at some of the places inside of you that you would rather ignore. Something amazing happens in patient Christianity when we look at our darkest places, because in the light of God's love we are liberated. It is a bittersweet experience, and there is nothing more fulfilling to the soul.

Patient Christianity is what Mary experienced and what her sister, Martha, missed (Luke 10:38–42). What are the key differences between these women that resulted in their different experiences of being with Jesus? Martha, we are told, welcomed Jesus into her home. Many of us have done the same. We have welcomed Jesus into our hearts. We realize there is something about Him and the promises He made that speak to the desires of our souls. Mary, on the other hand, sat at Jesus' feet. There seems to be a distinction here when it comes to devotion. Welcoming someone into your home and sitting at His feet are two different levels of devotion. Jesus invites each of us to the level Mary experienced. He wanted that for Martha as well. He appreciated her welcome, but He wanted so much more for her. He knew she could know Him better than that.

Sometimes simply welcoming Jesus can be hazardous to your spiritual health. Look at what we know of Martha. She was the head of a household, which probably meant that her husband had died. Having a home meant that she had a sense of responsibility to the guests who gathered there. We are told that she made many preparations and that these preparations became distractions. In fact, they distracted her so much that they built up resentment in her. Resentment reached the point that she complained to Jesus.

Has that ever happened to you? Have you ever welcomed Jesus so much that all the work involved has left you resentful? Women are especially vulnerable to this. We are the main workers in the church; we take care of the children and food while the men make the decisions. Martha was not only resentful of her sister, but she was also resentful of Jesus. She challenged Him, "Don't you care?" implying that He was a typical, insensitive male who failed to notice the unfair conditions under which she was serving. If you practice frantic Christianity, I'm sure you've wondered the same. I know I have.

Martha was also a worried person. She was deeply concerned about the state of her home, the comfort of the people present, and their physical needs. This worry and concern about so many things further blinded her from looking into Jesus' eyes. Martha's insecurity created the worry, resentment, and distraction that led her to welcome Jesus without being with Him.

Mary, on the other hand, moved beyond her resistances and let herself get closer to Jesus. She hung on to His every word. For Mary, Jesus' words rang louder and stronger than anything else in the room. What keeps us from being more like Mary?

Henri Nouwen asked, "Why is it so difficult to be still and quiet and let God speak to me about the meaning of my life? Is it because I don't trust God? Is it because I don't know God? Is it because I am afraid of God? Is it because everything else is more real for me than God? Is it because deep down, I do not believe that God cares?"[4]

If you responded, "Well, quite frankly, yes to all of the above," I challenge you to consider whether you have heard the voice of God. God doesn't shout at us; His voice is the quiet one we hear in our hearts. When we are worried, resentful, and burdened as Martha was, He says to us, "Come to Me, all who are weary and heavy-laden, and I will give you rest. Take my yoke upon you, and learn from Me, for I am gentle and humble in heart; and you shall find rest for your souls. For My yoke is easy, and My load is light" (Matt. 11:28–30).

Frantic Christianity comes naturally to women. Patient Christianity happens through the work of the Holy Spirit in a soul that releases itself to God. This process is deliberate, painful, and amazingly beneficial. Here are some steps you can take toward becoming a more patient Christian.

Steps to Becoming a Patient Christian

1. Spend Time with God

When we get beyond our franticness, just being still won't automatically resolve the turmoil in our souls. Stillness before God is something we must practice. It takes effort. In Psalm 46:10, God says to David, "Be still, and know that I am God"(NIV). Remember that David was a man after God's own heart. If anybody knew God, it was David. But his knowledge of God brought him to an urgent quest for stillness. He wouldn't get to know God better, he wouldn't keep moving toward Him, unless he found this place of stillness. It is so simple and yet so hard. Part of the simplicity is merely availability. You don't have to go to an exotic place, such as the top of Mount Everest or the center of Jerusalem to find this priceless gift. Exploring and discovering the heart of God is possible for anyone who comes to Him through Christ.

Once I was so overwhelmed with the trials in my life that I decided to have a talk with God. I poured myself a cup of tea, sat down at the kitchen table, and addressed God as if He were my best friend sitting there beside me. I can't remember any particular thought He gave me or much about our interaction that day, but I do remember the days that followed. Brian asked me what was different about me. My immediate reaction was "I don't know." I couldn't think of anything that had changed. After a minute or two, I remembered my tea time with God and realized that the experience had done something deep in my soul that I didn't even recognize. I've had many similar encounters with God since then.

I decided my prayer group could also benefit from this kind of fellowship with God. So once during our meeting together, I invited them to picture God in an empty chair at the center of our circle. I asked each woman to talk directly to Him about her needs and the needs of others in the room. It was a meaningful time. I have never experienced more laughter in a prayer meeting. Yet it was holy laughter, purified by a Savior who truly loves us and lives among us. Indeed, He could even have been giggling with us as we prayed. God is an easy companion.

2. Learn to Hear His Voice

I've discovered that during much of my Christian life I thought I was listening to the voice of God when what I was hearing was not at all a message from the throne of heaven. There is a major difference between God's voice and Satan's voice. Satan is the "accuser of our brethren" (Rev. 12:10). God always calls us by name, and there is no condemnation in His voice. Remembering that fact has helped me distinguish the voice of God from other voices. Jesus said that His sheep know His voice and follow Him (John 10:1–11). Why do sheep follow the voice of their shepherd? They know that the shepherd will protect them from predators, keep them from falling off cliffs, and lead them to fresh water and green pastures.

Animals are selective in distinguishing voices. For example, our dog, Happy, can tell the difference between my voice and Brian's. Unfortunately, Brian's relationship with him often involves necessary but unpleasant things, such as taking him to the vet and giving him a bath. So, sometimes when Brian calls for Happy, he hightails it for his doghouse and refuses to come out. Brian then asks me to call for him. Since Happy associates my voice with the one who feeds him, protects him from Benjamin, and takes him for walks, he comes right away. He responds to my voice because he trusts that I will be kind to him.

We need to view God in the same way in order to decipher His voice. When I sin, He doesn't say, "You did it again, Debi. I knew you would; you'll never conquer that." No. When I sin, He says, "Debi, Debi." Usually, that's all I need to hear. It's a kind and loving voice that calls me to repentance and restoration in Him (Rom. 2:4).

In much the same way, Jesus called Martha's name. When I first read the passages in Luke in which Jesus responded to Martha's complaint against her sister, I thought Jesus was irritated with her, speaking "Martha, Martha" like "Shame on you, you simple-minded fool." But as I looked deeper, I could almost hear Him saying, "Martha, [short pause] Martha! [more urgency]" He spoke her name twice because He wanted to get her attention. He knew how distracted, worried, and resentful she was. He knew she wouldn't immediately grasp His response to her. But He wanted to allow her the opportunity to hear what He had to say. "Martha. Listen to Me, Martha! There's something important I want to explain to you. I don't want you to miss it."

Jesus went on to speak of her sins. Yes, sins. She had welcomed Jesus, but now she was so busy serving Him that she had no time to be with Him. Serving God on our own terms is quite different from being with Him on His. Jesus didn't want bitterness and resentment clinging to Martha's soul, so He invited her to stop and receive the balm that would heal her.

3. Get Help When You Need It

Women are notorious for trying to do it all. I counsel many women who, though they work full-time, do all the housework even though they have able-bodied spouses. As women, we often struggle with the responsibility of having to fulfill so many roles.

After Faye agreed to say no to new demands made on her, her closest friend, Karen, underwent surgery. Faye was the obvious person to plan meals for Karen's family, but she didn't offer, so another friend, Joan, took on that job. When Joan left a message on Faye's answering machine asking her to make a meal one night, Faye felt paralyzed. She had promised the growth group that she would not take on any more responsibilities. Instead of calling Joan back immediately, she went to the group and explained the problem. Since Faye wanted to make a meal for her needy friend, the group agreed that as long as she asked someone to help her, she could do so. Faye hated the idea of imposing on anyone, but then she thought of Brenda. Brenda knew Karen. Privately, Faye asked Brenda to help with the meal, and Brenda eagerly agreed. Brenda is rarely asked to help in these ways at church. Her image as the has-it-all-together, single, career woman prevents people from considering her for these jobs. The next week Brenda talked about how much she had enjoyed helping their friend. Faye was surprised at how good it felt for both her and Brenda to help.

In the story of Mary and Martha, we never find out how Jesus thought all the work Martha was frantic about would get done. I have a thought. Unless Jesus planned to perform a miracle to feed the group, I think that after He finished speaking, He might have encouraged everyone (including the men) to work together to finish preparing the meal, meeting everyone's needs.

4. Start a Spiritual Workout Program

Beginning a new exercise program requires discipline and effort. When I decided to start jogging, I had to drag myself out of bed in the morning, pull on my sweats and sneakers, and force myself to go around the block. After a few weeks, however, I began to look forward to getting up, and instead of going around one block, I was going around several. I also noticed that I had more energy to get me through the day.

The same is true of spiritual workouts. It takes determination and effort to seek spiritual growth. But as you spend time reflecting on God's Word, you'll begin to notice positive changes: You'll be more at peace, have more patience, and have more emotional strength to deal with the stresses of life.

In this section, I want to suggest a few spiritual disciplines you can do to exercise your soul. (You can learn more about these disciplines in Richard Foster's book *Celebration of the Disciplines*.)

Inward Disciplines

• *Meditation*—This involves memorizing and reflecting on short passages of Scripture and asking God what He has to tell you through them. The more I have meditated on Genesis 1–3, the basis of this book, the more insights I have received. I've memorized most of the passages, without specifically deciding to do that. It's as if these passages have become a part of me, they are so deeply ingrained in my brain.

• *Prayer*—Prayer is a *two-way* conversation with God. It involves listening, attentiveness, and communion. It is actually enjoying the privilege of God's presence. Sometimes it goes beyond human words and thoughts (Rom. 8:26–27). We can pray anytime, anywhere, about anything. It is not poetic words that turn the heart of heaven in our direction; rather, it is a sincere and contrite heart.

• *Fasting*—In my own life, I have practiced fasting when I had to make an important decision and wanted to be sure I heard God's voice. A fast doesn't have to mean abstinence from food. You can abstain from watching TV, for example. Whatever you abstain from, the purpose of fasting is to tune in to God and His love and to invite Him more deeply into your life.

• *Study*—Studying the Bible is different from meditating upon it. When you meditate upon the Bible, you are seeking to understand what God may be saying to you personally. When you study the Bible, you are more focused on understanding what God is saying to everyone. You examine the context of the passage; you consult with other scholars. You seek to understand as best you can the original intention of the passage. I really appreciate the efforts of Precepts Ministries, Bible Study Fellowship, and others in their disciplined efforts to help women study the Word of God. Of course, in study, we do see our own lives, and God speaks to us there. However, the intention of this discipline is to correctly handle the Word of truth as instructed in 2 Timothy 2:15.

Outward Disciplines

• *Simplicity*—This is a spiritual discipline we women should practice more. If we looked in our closets right now, how many pairs of shoes would we find? What about outfits? How many "toys," such as stereos, TV sets, and cars, do we have that we could easily do without?

After my first garage sale, I couldn't believe the junk I had gotten rid of. Anything that didn't sell went to Goodwill. I removed a couple of truckloads of articles from my house that day. But when I returned, I realized that this was only the tip of the iceberg. Oh, how I long to follow God's direction of simplicity! Once He led me not to buy clothes for myself for a whole calendar year. It was a wonderful experience. It was special to receive gifts of clothes that year and really enjoy them in a way I would not have otherwise.

We can also simplify our eating habits. God might lead you to eat out less and save that money to share with a food pantry. We might be led to simplicity in entertaining, focusing more on the fellowship between believers in our homes than on expensive china and the perfect table setting. (Sorry, Martha Stewart.)

Invite God to lead you down the path of simplicity. Don't do it by your own effort. God leads us to the discipline of simplicity when we recognize that all of our material possessions can't compare to a relationship with Him.

• *Solitude*—This may be a scary word to some readers. Women define themselves so tightly by their relationships that some may fear being alone. Solitude is the complete opposite of loneliness. Loneliness can exist in the middle of a crowd. For solitude, it is necessary to be away from eye contact and conversation with other human beings. It is the discipline of being with God. It has no agenda. It is listening and abiding with the One who loves us. It is during these periods of solitude that we are changed in our countenances, our values, our beliefs, our endurance. It isn't a change of our own making. Our part is to choose to spend this time with God. I enjoy times of solitude as I take a nature walk. Sometimes I bring along my Bible or another book that leads me on a reflective exercise. Sometimes I look up at the clouds and wonder at the beauty of my Creator.

• *Submission*—Here's another unpopular word in the world today. Submission is the discipline of letting go. It is giving God control of our lives and willingly obeying whatever He calls us to do, whether that means keeping our mouths shut when we think we have the answer or forgiving someone who hurt us deeply. Obedience's outward action will differ for each circumstance and situation. But it has the same internal motivator: a mustard seed of faith in the God who called us to it.

• *Service*—When service is a spiritual discipline, there is nothing so rewarding to a heart. We won't need to be recognized. In fact, we will yearn to be anonymous because our service becomes a privileged opportunity to participate with God in His work. It won't be our idea, our effort, or our gifts. It will be our moment to lay another crown before our deserving King. We serve God because we love Him, and we realize that serving Him is a privilege. We are not trying to settle our debt to Him through serving Him because Christ has paid off that debt completely. Rather, service to God is simply the response of a grateful heart.

Corporate Disciplines

• *Confession*—Here's a spiritual discipline that we don't often see practiced in daily life or corporate worship in many churches. There is a beautiful spirit that accompanies a meeting of believers who join in support of one another as they practice public confession. On the rare occasions I have experienced this discipline in the body of Christ, judgments and gossip were stifled by the beauty of sinners admitting their needs. No one feels immune from sin when confronted by Jesus' words: "He who is without sin among you, let him be the first to throw a stone . . ." (John 8:7).

• *Worship*—How grateful I am to the hymn writers who speak words of worship that I'm not sure I would utter on my own. "Crown Him with Many Crowns" and "Holy, Holy, Holy" are two of the hymns that help me picture God as I worship. There is nothing like worship with other believers as we experience His presence in our midst.

• *Guidance*—As we look into God's Word together, we receive guidance and instruction for our lives. We learn from the Word and from one another what God has to teach us. We receive guidance from pastors, friends, and mentors. We need direction for our lives from godly people.

My daughter is often perplexed by why we have to sit and listen to a sermon on Sunday mornings at church. She enjoys singing and being sung to, but she dreads the lengthy lesson from Scripture. I remember being a young girl and wondering the same thing. When the Word of God is offered in corporate worship, it is done to remind us of God's love for us and to give us direction for our lives. It is an opportunity to praise and worship God, who communes with us through His Word.

• *Celebration*—Celebrating the joy of knowing God with other believers stimulates our souls and prepares us for the joy of heaven. We can worship and praise God in the privacy of our own homes, but it hardly compares with corporate celebration. My husband called me on his cellular phone from Boulder, Colorado, one evening during a Promise Keepers rally. He was in the midst of 50,000 men, all singing praises to God. He didn't want me to miss out on the celebration he was experiencing.

Other Disciplines

Another avenue of spiritual growth is reading spiritual books. I have found deep comfort and even friendship from men and women who lived hundreds of years ago. The words they left behind have led me to a deeper relationship with Jesus. I think every Christian should read *The Pursuit of God* by A. W. Tozer. Another important Christian classic is *The Imitation of Christ* by Thomas à Kempis.

We can also find peace by going on spiritual retreats, finding someone to be our spiritual director, and asking someone to disciple us.

Something I have found helpful in addressing franticness is to take Sundays off. When I discipline myself not to catch up on work and other things on Sundays, I enjoy my week much more.

Keeping a prayer journal has been an important method of spiritual growth for me. I am often amazed at how my journal entries minister to me as I reread them.

Time for You

What are some spiritual disciplines you can practice to help you grow spiritually?

His Power Is Made Perfect in Our Weakness

We will be constantly tempted toward franticness and away from God. When I read the temptation of Christ (Luke 4:1–13), I think, *What a proud moment that was for God the Father!* Here was His Son being tempted in all the ways that we are and that Adam and Eve were and trusting so completely in the character of the Father that He stopped Satan in his tracks.

On the days I'm disgusted with myself for really blowing it, I'm tempted to listen to that voice that tells me to give up. Then I admit, "God, I've really blown it now. I need You more than ever." There's nothing that pleases Him more. He doesn't want me to try to be the best person in the world in my own strength. He longs for me to realize my limitations and come to Him just as I am. When I admit my weakness and brokenness, only then am I truly strong, just as Paul said (2 Cor. 12:10).

CHAPTER SIXTEEN

Understanding Men

T hank God for men! After all, it was He who created them. I wholeheartedly believe that while there's nothing like a woman, there's also nothing like a man. Think about what life would be like without men. It would be empty and boring, in my opinion.

Men and Genesis

In this chapter, we'll look at men in general and husbands specifically. So, if you don't have a husband, this chapter will give you a perspective on marriage, as well as help you understand some of the men who inhabit your world.

Of course we need to go right back to Genesis to get a glimpse of how God created man in order to answer the question "How do I live with a man?" In the Bible, the first mention of a man was in Genesis 2:5 in the context of performing a task, specifically cultivating plants. The first mention of a woman was in Genesis 2:18 in the context of relationship.

Scholars disagree on whether Adam was given greater responsibility for the relationship between him and Eve before the fall. In my opinion, there appears to be a headship among equals. I think Adam was held slightly more responsible than Eve for several reasons. First, the command not to eat of the tree of knowledge of good and evil was given to Adam before Eve was created (Gen. 2:16–17). In Genesis 3:3, during Eve's conversation with the serpent, she refers to the tree in the middle of the garden, not specifically mentioning the tree of the knowledge of good and evil. It could be that Eve was given this information secondhand by Adam. The other evidence of a headship among equals is found in Genesis 3:7, when their eyes were opened only *after* the man ate.

This headship in their relationship fades in light of the equality and unity they shared. Headship among equals is demonstrated in a good business relationship. Adam, being slightly more responsible, would be similar to a president, and Eve would be the vice president. In the corporate world, if a president went around emphasizing his greater responsibility to the vice president, it wouldn't make for a good relationship that would allow both to contribute. In a successful corporation, both officers feel their opinions and input are valuable, but they understand that the greater responsibility and greater decision-making power belong to the president and that the latter is used rarely or in deadlocked situations. The emphasis in Adam and Eve's relationship appears to be on needing each other and becoming one, much more than on headship. But it appears that the equality, oneness, and unity were achieved through a headship among equals.

In Genesis 3:6, we observe the man's tendency toward passivity and withdrawal. The moment that the foundations of the universe were being tested, Adam observed silently without taking action. He simply stood by and watched as Eve first ate the forbidden fruit.

In Genesis 3:12, we also see Adam's (and later Eve's) tendency to blame. When Adam responded to God's question "Who told you that you were naked?" he resorted to blaming Eve and even God Himself by stating, "The *woman* that *You* gave me" (paraphrase mine).

All of this information from Genesis shows me that the man's cycle of damaging relationships differs slightly from the woman's.

Man's Cycle of Damaging Relationships

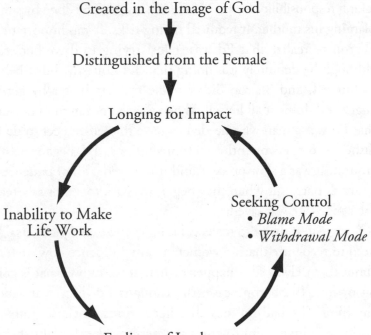

Created in the Image of God

↓

Distinguished from the Female

↓

Longing for Impact

Inability to Make
Life Work

Seeking Control
• *Blame Mode*
• *Withdrawal Mode*

Feelings of Inadequacy

During their counseling, Sharon and Ed could better see how Ed had let Sharon do it all and how she threatened his sense of adequacy. Ed was born with a longing to be loved, just as Sharon was, but he also needed to have some impact on his world. He didn't come from a broken home as Sharon did; in fact, his parents are still married to this day. He was raised by a mother who thought he was the center of the universe. She showed little respect for his father, but she did everything for Ed. This led to Ed's tendency toward withdrawal. His mother's treatment of him left him believing that he was incapable of doing much on his own. She was still cutting his meat for him when he was 12. So it wasn't surprising that he married a woman who could do it all.

For Ed, getting off the cycle of damaging relationships meant taking responsibility for his own life. It couldn't be done by simply blaming his mother. It required taking risks. It was important for Sharon to realize that Ed wasn't just trying to drive her crazy, although he definitely was doing that. Ed honestly didn't believe in himself, and Sharon didn't make matters better by getting angry and doing it all herself. When Sharon began to understand that Ed was a man who needed to have the self-respect to do the dishes and take on other responsibilities, Ed began to turn around. It was a slow process, and it required a lot of patience on Sharon's part, but when they began to work together as a team, their marriage was saved.

The greatest threat to maleness is femaleness, and vice versa. We need to recognize that we women greatly influence how men feel about themselves. This happens whether we know what is going on or not. In Sharon's case, she thought Ed didn't care about anything. She had no idea that her actions all those years did nothing to invite him to grow as a person. She thought she was being the best possible wife for Ed.

The greatest moment in Sharon's marriage was the day Ed made a public profession of his faith by joining the church. As it turned out, he had made a decision for Christ many years earlier while watching a Billy Graham crusade on TV. He had never had the courage to share this with Sharon because he didn't want to bring up one more area in which she outshone him and knew everything there was to know. Sharon told him that she felt like a baby Christian, too, and suggested that maybe they could learn more about God together.

There's Nothing Like a Man

Brenda had been so threatened by men all of her life that she had never been close enough to one to understand them. She found that feeling rejected by her father was one of her reasons for always keeping men at a distance. At first she had a hard time recognizing how her "got it all together, don't need you" walls kept men away.

Studying man's cycle of damaging relationships expanded her understanding of her father. She saw him stuck in the blame mode, creating distance from his wife and daughter so he wouldn't be seen as inadequate. Brenda started looking at the men at work differently. She had done most of the hiring at her job, and since she didn't relate well to men, most of her subordinates were women. There was one man, Mike, who was working in an entry-level position.

Brenda decided to try an experiment and treat Mike a little differently. While she developed rapport with the other women by opening herself up to their confidences, she sought ways to talk to Mike about his impact in the office. She found opportunities to encourage him for the way he carried out tasks. The craziest thing happened. As Brenda approached him differently, he opened up to her and even shared about his personal relationships. It improved the whole atmosphere at work. Now all the women included Mike in office discussions and looked to him for a male perspective. The office was a more pleasant place to work because of this newfound camaraderie.

During the years Brenda had blocked men out of her life, she really didn't know that they have important and valuable contributions to make.

Men and Women Are Different

Men and women apply different perspectives to problems. When both of these perspectives are respected and considered, usually the best decisions are made. Whether the decisions are made by married partners, church committees, or business executives, the male and female perspectives together expose dimensions neither sees alone.

To guide us to a better understanding of men, I want to highlight four major areas where men's and women's perspectives differ.

Men's Greatest Fear Is Failure

From boyhood, a man is conditioned to avoid failure. Just as a girl's greatest pain is centered in her relationships, a boy's greatest pain is centered in his inadequacies. A woman defines herself by her relationships, and a man defines himself by his accomplishments. He fears failure in sports, school, and other undertakings. He is conditioned to believe that he is supposed to be strong, to always have the answers, to be independent, and to know the way without asking for help. Well, we women know very well that all men fail us. We can do much to help them understand and grow from their failures if we break away from the pressure we put on them not to fail us.

Fairy tales like *Cinderella* only further complicate the relationship between a man and a woman. Through them, a girl is conditioned to believe that one day a man will come into her life, that he will never fail her, and that they will live happily ever after. We must give men room to fail and always call them back to be the best they can possibly be. When we hold to the expectation that a man must succeed in every regard every time, we drive that man further from us. As you respond to your man with encouragement, forgiveness, and a firm belief in him, you will have a great impact on his life.

Faye unknowingly had become a wonderful example in calling her husband, Jack, to greatness. He didn't believe in himself when they were first married. But her gentle, consistent, and determined love pierced his soul and gave him a confidence he never had before. The chronically out-of-work auto mechanic became a respected business owner and community leader.

Let me share this wonderful story from the life of an American pastor's wife. She was Jane Hill, the wife of E. V. Hill, the pastor of Mount Zion Missionary Baptist Church in Los Angeles. E. V. tearfully shared this story at Jane's funeral. James Dobson wrote about it in a newsletter. Dr. Dobson said:

> As a struggling young preacher, E. V. had trouble earning a living. That led him to invest the family's scarce resources, over Jane's objections, in the purchase of a service station. She felt her husband lacked the time and expertise to oversee his investment, which proved to be accurate. Eventually, the station went broke and E. V. lost his shirt in the deal.
>
> E. V. came home that night expecting his wife to be pouting over his foolish investment. Instead, she sat down with him and said, "I've been doing some figuring. I figure that you don't smoke and you don't drink. If you smoked and drank, you would have lost as much as you lost in the service station. So, it's six in one hand and a half-dozen in the other. Let's forget it."
>
> Shortly after the fiasco with the service station, E. V. came home one night and found the house dark. When he opened the door, he saw that Jane had prepared a candlelight dinner for two. E. V. thought that was a great idea and went into the bathroom to wash his hands. He tried unsuccessfully to turn

on the light. Then he felt his way into the bedroom and flipped another switch. Darkness prevailed. The young pastor went back to the dining room and asked Jane why the electricity was off. She began to cry.

"You work so hard, and we're trying," said Jane, "but it's pretty rough. I didn't have quite enough money to pay the light bill. I didn't want you to know about it, so I thought we would just eat by candlelight." [1]

Like Jane Hill, we all have a deep impact on the men to whom we are closest. How we respond to their failures has the power to tear them down or build them up.

Men Are More Aggressive Than Women

Hormones affect men and women differently. Men and women both produce testosterone and estrogen. The amount and proportions vary greatly. Men produce some estrogen, but it occurs in much higher amounts in women. In women, estrogen fluctuates with the monthly cycle—in fact, it helps control the cycle—and contributes to mood swings. In turn, women produce some testosterone, but it is primarily a male hormone and is found in higher amounts in men. Testosterone affects aggression. Basically, the man is chemically better suited to act in aggressive and angry ways. Part of his conditioning against admitting failure will lead him to believe that tears, hurt, or fear is a weakness that might produce or magnify failure.

The fear of failure (or loss of face, which is failure of a sort) is a major factor in influencing a man's aggression as well. When he feels shame or inadequacy, he might try to overpower these negative emotions with aggression and anger. He is more comfortable with aggression than he is with shame. This moves him along the cycle to blame in order to avoid the pain of inadequacy. Most men repress their sense of shame and inadequacy, so they don't recognize how much those factors affect the ways they relate in the world.

Women have a useful opportunity here to call men to accountability about their aggressiveness. In this way, we call them to greatness. A truly successful man learns how to control and manage his natural tendencies toward aggression rather than allowing them to hurt himself and others.

It is mandatory that women maintain appropriate boundaries when it comes to men's aggressive behavior. A woman is not responsible for the way a man manages his anger, but she is responsible for how she receives the anger. She should not allow his anger to be detrimental to their relationship. She needs to hold him accountable for dealing with this God-given aspect of his personality.

The woman is not at fault for a man's violence. In every occasion of physical abuse of which I'm aware, the man insists that the woman is responsible. If only she had said something else or behaved differently, he would not have lost his temper. That is patently false. At all times, the man is responsible for his own actions, for exploding or for abstaining from violence.

In fact, a woman can become a part of the cycle of violence if she believes that she is responsible for her husband's behavior. If there is violence in your home, it is important for you to break the cycle by not tolerating the behavior. You need to call the police and seek shelter and counseling. Your husband (or boyfriend) needs to take responsibility for his violence and learn how to control his anger.

Men Are More Logical Than Women

Men's left-brain, straight-line logic often gives them an unemotional perspective on situations. Much of the marriage counseling that I do focuses on helping wives recognize that their husbands don't think the same way they do. Women expect men to have the same emotional makeup as women, or at least an emotional makeup that women can understand.

It is important for women to respect this part of men (even though it drives us crazy at times). When a woman is willing to see the logical perspective, she might be better able to invite a man to listen to the emotional perspective. Men are emotional beings, but they need time, patience, and help in identifying and expressing their emotions.

Sharon's pattern with Ed in the past was to get more and more upset with Ed when he didn't follow through with what she asked him to do. Usually, she would display her anger. Sometimes she was so desperate that she would break into tears. It all had the same effect on Ed—he simply ignored her and did what he wanted.

Sharon communicated best with Ed when she firmly laid out the facts and left it at that. For instance, it was Ed's job to take his hunting dogs to the vet for shots. In the past, Sharon would nag Ed for a couple of weeks, have an emotional display, and in the end take the dogs herself. This year she sat down and looked Ed in the eye.

In a calm voice, she said, "Ed, I know in the past I have reminded you to take your dogs for shots and then I've taken them myself. This year is different. I'm only going to say this once. It's time for the dogs to go, but I am not going to take them. If you don't take them and one gets sick, it will break my heart. It may also put you and our neighborhood at risk, but I will not be taking them this year."

Ed nodded, and that was all that was said. Sharon fought herself for a whole week, desperate to remind Ed or to show some emotional display to get his attention. But she didn't.

A week later, Ed took the dogs. Sharon was elated. Respectfully talking to Ed on his terms had gotten through to him.

Men Are Sexual Beings

My husband says that the way sex influences a man's behavior and thinking is difficult for a woman to fully understand and relate to. Men are conditioned to believe that manhood is sexuality, and they see themselves as powerful when they are sexual. This can be threatening, frightening, and frustrating for women. A woman can accept that a man is different from her and do what she can in the way she dresses and interacts with him to make his battle less difficult. A woman must not take responsibility for a man's sexual struggles; only he can overcome his temptations through Christ. Women can be sensitive to this struggle in men without taking responsibility for it.

As in the case of aggression, it is important for a woman to draw distinct boundaries. A woman is not responsible for a man's mistreatment of her. He must control his own sexual nature. In marriage, a man receives different benefits from a sexual relationship. Men might misuse sex as a way to get relief. Women, on the other hand, might misuse sex as a reward: "If you do this for me, I'll make you happy tonight." Neither of these ways is healthy. Sexuality in marriage is for the purpose of giving and receiving pleasure. Using sex as a reward or for relief cheapens it and denies its original purpose of representing oneness and closeness in the relationship. We can help men by understanding their unique sexual nature and inviting them to relate to us in a way that honors God.

Regina remembered a time she felt totally used by her husband, Mike. It was during those early years of marriage when she was trying to be a model Christian woman. She came across 1 Corinthians 7:5 in which Paul tells married couples not to deny their spouses sexual pleasure. Regina interpreted that to mean that if Mike was in the mood, it would be like breaking one of the Ten Commandments to say no. Mike wasn't bothered by Regina's behavior at all, and he enjoyed her anytime-anywhere attitude. But Regina was building up resentment. When she talked to Mike about it, he told her that he wanted to make love when *she* wanted.

Calling Men to Greatness

Some people might argue that men are the way they are by nature. Since their hormones and brain function make them more fearful of failure, more aggressive, more sexual, and more logical, why not let them be the way they were created to be? John Trent and Gary Smalley have a good answer to that question. "As believers, we never were called to be 'natural' men but spiritual men—men of God who have a lower (human) nature but a higher calling."[2]

As women we have a unique opportunity to call the men in our lives to greatness. We do this as our nature exposes how men's natural way of being is not healthy and needs the Holy Spirit's power to transform them for intimate relationships. In our accepting presence, our men can learn to risk failure. They will find that they need to go deeper emotionally, beyond their natural anger and aggression, to meet us emotionally and find unity. They will also perceive that having great sex involves nurturing and pleasing their wives, not just satisfying themselves. They will discover that their logical thinking is valuable but also limiting at times, especially when figuring out relationships. Our relationships with men are what call them to greatness. We invite them to become the men God means for them to be.

Living with a Man in Marriage

When we get married, something happens to us women that we don't expect: We become more vulnerable to pain. You don't have to be married long before you discover this reality. The pain comes from realizing that our husbands will not completely meet our love need. It is a necessary pain that if accepted, grieved over, and embraced will lead us closer together.

Early in our marriage, Brian and I took a personality test. The results showed that Brian viewed me as undisciplined. I couldn't believe it. Here I was, a graduate student who had never turned an assignment in late, who worked full-time in a self-motivating position and part-time as a Christian counselor, who made dinner every night (however unappetizing it may have been), and he thought I was undisciplined because I left my shoes where I took them off and I didn't do the dirty dishes right away. At first I set out to show him he was wrong by proving how disciplined I was. This was my way of trying to resolve that pain. But through the years, I've come to realize that Brian can only accept me incompletely. Try as he might, Brian may never be completely free of his own beliefs and standards and will always judge me on some level. Rather than focusing on trying to change Brian, I have accepted this about him. This frees me from the power that the pain of feeling rejected by my husband can have in driving me to make unhealthy choices.

Women can go to extremes trying to extract the love they want from the men in their lives. The *Dallas Morning News* carried an article titled "Husband Stabbed Over Cost of Valentine's Flowers, Police Say."[3] Now there's a woman who wanted to get her point across (no pun intended). Women in Austria are looking to the government to help them straighten out their wayward spouses. They are seeking legislation that would require husbands to share in child-rearing and household responsibilities.[4]

When women use controlling, demanding means to mold their husbands into the men they want them to be, women can make themselves miserable in marriage. In fact, marriage seems to benefit men more than women. Married men significantly outlive unmarried men, but the same is not true of married women.[5]

Evidently, this quest to try to make our husbands into what we think they should be isn't new. King Solomon had interesting ways of describing women:

> "It is better to live in a desert land, than with a contentious and vexing woman" (Prov. 21:19).

> "It is better to live in a corner of the roof than in a house shared with a contentious woman" (Prov. 25:24).

> "A constant dripping on a day of steady rain and a contentious woman are alike" (Prov. 27:15).

These statements are from a man with 700 wives.

I don't like to hear these verses quoted to me by men, but I do think they help women understand the impact we can have on the males in our lives. Remember Proverbs 14:1: "The wise woman builds her house, but the foolish [woman] tears it down with her own hands." All women are after the same thing: They want to be loved by their men. Only, the wise woman recognizes that she has the power to tear down her home or build it up.

My husband, colleagues, and I wrote *Passages of Marriage* because we saw people repeatedly making the same mistakes in their marriages, and we wanted to describe the ordinary issues all couples need to resolve. We all face difficulties in marriage having to do with control and power struggles, dealing with in-laws, adjusting to children, and coping with losses.

How do we avoid common mistakes in our marriages? After considerable experience in the field of marriage counseling, I have identified four core principles we need to center on in order to be happy in marriage.

Four Ways to Build a Happy Marriage

1. Understand Submission

I believe that misunderstanding the concepts of submission and forgiveness has done more damage to Christians' souls and relationships than any other issue.

My own story shows how easy it is to be misdirected. When I got married, I was in seminary. I had studied the Scripture passages about submission in marriage and had decided that the best way to ensure a perfect relationship was by being submissive. Brian and I were living in a two-bedroom apartment in Indiana. It had one heating unit in the living room; to heat the other rooms, we had to keep all the doors open. It was that kind of a place.

One day shortly after we were married, Brian was studying in the room that served as our office/study. I was in the kitchen writing thank-you notes and listening to a tape. Suddenly, Brian yelled from the other room, "Can you turn down that music?" I turned it down. Then he yelled again: "I can still hear it." I turned it so low that I could barely hear it. A third time he yelled: "Please turn it down." I finally just turned it off.

It was about this time that I asked Brian, "Are you happy in our marriage?"

"Yes, very." He looked surprised that I would think there could possibly be any other answer.

"Well, I'm not very happy," I said.

In a way, I was pleased that what I had been doing was making him happy. And from his point of view, it was certainly nice that I did everything he told me without question. But what would have happened if this had continued for a long time? In the first three months, he didn't do anything that could be construed as verbally, psychologically, or spiritually abusive. But would he have, if I had not held him accountable?

That night, we sat down and had a long talk. He didn't make a lot of changes at first, but I changed a lot. I began to express my feelings and opinions. I even openly disagreed with him at times. When our first anniversary arrived, we were studying together with the TV on. A year before, he wouldn't have believed he could do that. That's when I realized that speaking my opinions was good for him.

To understand submission, we need a clear definition of what submission is and what it isn't.

- Submission IS NOT doing what you're told and keeping quiet.

- Submission IS an attitude of respect (for the dignity of being created in God's image and our potential in Christ); an attitude of trust in God, not in one's husband; and an attitude of considering someone else's point of view.

Through the years, I've learned that being submissive to Brian involves much more than simply doing things his way. It involves wrestling with my own desire for self-protection and lack of forgiveness. I've learned that being submissive to Brian sometimes means being quiet and listening, sometimes means confronting him with his sin, and sometimes means being firm about how I see things, but it always means recognizing and respecting that he is the man God planned for me to spend my life with.

In my years of marriage and marriage counseling, I've found that the way to a man's heart isn't through his stomach. The way to a man's heart is through respect. Ephesians 5:33 is a great verse that summarizes the understanding I attempt to instill in couples. I teach a man how to love his wife and a wife how to respect her husband.

Although I hate the way some well-meaning Christians have overemphasized submission to the detriment of many men and women, I believe that this virtue is important and beautiful. I appreciate Thomas à Kempis's description of it:

> It is an indication that you still love yourself too much if you are afraid to submit to others. What a paltry comparison if you, nothing but ashes, submit yourself to others in the Lord, when I the Almighty and most high God, the Creator of everything, subjected myself to the world for your sake! I became the most humble and submissive of all people, that you might overcome your pride with my humility.[6]

You have a unique place in your husband's life. You can blind yourself to his wrong behavior or you can call him to greatness. In a good marriage, as in a good friendship, "iron sharpens iron" (Prov. 27:17). When you see your husband falling in certain areas, you can help him grow.

Of course, it is totally appropriate for a husband to perform the same role for his wife. But this is a book for women living with men. I am examining the woman's role. Just remember that at its best, it works both ways.

2. Build a Strong Spiritual Base

Nothing has kept me more committed to an imperfect man than my commitment to God. Sometimes loving Brian seems impossible. Looking at him, sleeping with him, and being with him can be maddening when he has hurt me or been insensitive to my needs. When he hasn't come through for me in a way that I think he must, I can get irritated. It's then that Solomon's descriptions of a quarrelsome woman apply to me.

This is where a strong spiritual base comes in. Brian and I both agree that we would not be married today if it weren't for our individual relationships with God. The times I don't *want* to be married to Brian because he has said or done something that makes me dislike him are the times I *choose* to be married to him because the God who loves me tells me to stay. My commitment to Brian is a covenant I have made with God.

Your Covenant Is with God

You need to see your marriage vows as a covenant with God and not with your husband. When you view marriage this way, you are less likely to sever your vows based on what your husband does. You are promising God you will love, honor, and cherish your husband whether he deserves it or not.

One day we will all stand before the judgment seat. As we face God, He will remind us, "I gave you that husband to love. How did you do?" We need to recognize the immense ministry that we are given right in our own homes with our own husbands.

The Holy Spirit Is Your Guide

The Holy Spirit's guidance keeps Brian and me together. And if I would only listen to the Holy Spirit sooner, I would not lose as much sleep as I do. Many times Brian and I have stayed up late fighting, only to end up apologizing. Yet, earlier in the fight, the Holy Spirit told me to take responsibility for what I had done wrong. If I had done that immediately, healing would have occurred much sooner and with less pain. Too often I choose the other path, focusing on and complaining about Brian's offenses in the matter.

Don't Underestimate the Power of Your Prayers

Ephesians 3:14–15 says, "For this reason, I bow my knees before the Father, from whom every family in heaven and on earth derives its name." The family that Brian and I created when we were married derives its name from God. It was God who first created families. Therefore, we need to recognize His interest in our family as we make decisions regarding it.

Peter, a married apostle, was guided by the Holy Spirit to give women who long to have spiritual influence on their husbands some vital advice. First Peter 3:1–2 says, "In the same way, you wives, be submissive to your own husbands so that even if any of them are disobedient to the word, they may be won without a word by the behavior of their wives, as they observe your chaste and respectful behavior." Wives need to pray more and nag less. I pray for my husband every day. My prayers have rarely yielded instant results, but over time, it's the fervent prayer of a righteous woman (James 5:16) that gets the job done. I pray about things in my husband's life that I think need changing. Some things I pray about for years. For example, Brian asked me to pray about his weight. I agreed, but I didn't have much faith in that prayer because I didn't see him making any effort to lose weight. I didn't fully understand what a battle it was for him and how he thought about it every day. I simply prayed. About two years later, he lost 60 pounds. He says my prayers laid the groundwork for this accomplishment.

Do you pray for your husband each day? You have a unique opportunity to be a spiritual partner with him whether he is a Christian or not.

3. Find a Support Group

Never underestimate the power of a good friend to help you love your man. In fact, you should choose friends who are committed to their own marriages, or to the concept of marriage, and will encourage you in your struggle to live with and love an imperfect person. Heaven knows it is not an easy thing to do.

I once met a friend for lunch. She looked discouraged—really at the end of her rope. She confessed to me, "Debi, I just don't know if I love him anymore. I never thought I could say something like that. I feel awful and hopeless."

I looked her in the eye and said, "I know exactly how you feel, because I've felt the same way."

After she recovered from her shock at my response, we continued our conversation. We talked about the fight that had precipitated her revelation. I didn't offer solutions for easily resolving the conflict. Instead I gave her a chance to see that in my own marriage, I have faced similar roadblocks and have successfully overcome them. As we went our separate ways, I noticed that she had a smile on her face and walked with a lighter step. Nothing about her relationship with her husband had changed. She hadn't seen him or talked to him. But her perspective had changed because she talked it over with a friend.

Another woman might be able to see some of your husband's positive qualities that you can't see. For example, Regina was complaining about Mike's new obsession with budgeting. Their kids were getting older, and Mike and Regina were trying to prepare for college. Mike wanted Regina to save every receipt, and it was driving her crazy. Sharon told Regina that budgeting was a good idea and that she should give it a try. That helped Regina put Mike's request in perspective.

4. Respect Your Husband

Respect takes many forms. In any form, it calls the husband to accountability. For example, if he is being abusive, respect is saying, "I know you can do better than that, so I won't enable it."

Mindlessly accepting his abuse is not respect, either for him or for yourself. Calling his simple ignorance or insensitivity "abuse" is just as disrespectful and doesn't get you anywhere. You should do what you can do, with discernment.

You should not do anything for your husband that contradicts God's Word—lying on income tax returns, stealing, and enabling drug or alcohol addiction, for example.

Sharon frequently wondered whether she should or could respect Ed. So she made a list (she's one of those people who love lists) that she would review during the many times she struggled to respect him. Here it is:

1. Tell God you are powerless to respect on your own— rely on the Holy Spirit.

2. Respect the leadership that he is supposed to be bringing, and pray that he will bring it.

3. Grieve through your hurt and pain—forgive!

4. Confront in love—don't nag.

5. Hang on for the ride.

6. Have lots of good friends to lean on and love.

Some Final Words of Advice

How to Deenergize Your Man

- Constantly tell him how he could be doing better and making more money.

- Constantly compare him with your father or other men.

- Put your children before him, and never give him attention.

- Expect him to meet all of your needs, and complain when he doesn't.

- Use sex as a reward, and withhold it as punishment.

How to Energize Your Man

- Regularly remind him of your commitment and love.

- Give your marriage priority over your children.

- Believe that he is doing his best, and stand beside him (pray, pray, pray!).

- Make special efforts to know what pleases him, and do those things regularly.

- Respect him by esteeming him, showing him consideration and appreciation, and courteously listening to his opinions, wishes, and judgments.

Time for You

Has your husband ever told you about a time you energized him? Describe that time and what you did.

Marriage is one of the awesome ministries many of us are privileged to be involved in during our journey on earth. As with all ministries, success depends on relying on God. As we abide in Christ—the Vine (John 15:1)—we receive a vision, purpose, and pathway for fulfilling this ministry in our men's lives.

CHAPTER SEVENTEEN

The Feminine Physique

D iane came bounding into the growth group, late again. In her usual way, she infected the group with whatever mood she was in. "Bathing suit season" and a roll of her eyes said it all to the women gathered there.

"I signed the kids up for swimming lessons, and one of the requirements is that I get in the water with them," she said. "What is it about buying a bathing suit that makes me so depressed?"

Judy looked with longing at Diane's svelte figure and couldn't understand what she had to complain about. *Look at her! Diane has the type of body bathing suits are made for.*

Faye thought about her problems finding a bathing suit that is modest enough without looking like it was made in 1938. The bathing suits featured in the *Sports Illustrated* swimsuit issue were not exactly her cup of tea.

Brenda didn't have to worry about bathing suits anymore. She had been able to structure her life to avoid wearing one. She didn't have children to ferry to a pool, and she simply skipped social settings in which bathing suits were expected or required.

Joy purchased about 10 bathing suits a season so that on any given day, she had at least one that emphasized what she believed to be her good features and deemphasized the others. For her, a bathing suit wasn't something to swim in; it was a fashion statement. But it didn't make her enjoy bathing suit season any more than the other women did. It was just another mandatory dictum, like everything else in her life.

Sharon couldn't care less about swimsuits. She wore one when she needed to and gave little thought to it. She was about the only one unaffected by the conversation, so she was ready to move it in a more interesting direction.

That was when Regina said, "You know, I think that the matter Diane has raised is important to consider when we're in the process of growing into our true feminine identity. Our feminine souls are garaged in feminine bodies. We haven't talked much about our bodies. How do you think God wants us to feel about bathing suit season?"

Time for You

How do you think God wants you to feel about bathing suit season or about your body specifically?

A book about women would not be complete without a discussion of the confusing, conflicting, and complicated side of our femininity: our bodies and our sexuality. How should we view our bodies? What is God's design for sexuality? How should single women approach sex? What is sexual abuse? The answers to these questions have important implications for our femininity.

We've studied Genesis 1–3 to improve our understanding of our identity as women. Genesis 2:24–25 mentions our sexuality in the context of nakedness. Do you realize that God created us for nakedness? Many of us probably cringe at that thought. The last place we want to be is naked in front of the world. But too many of us are carrying around a body loathing that is offensive to our souls. While we live here on earth, we exist in both body and soul.

Body Loathing

Sit down with a group of women for more than 30 minutes, and sooner or later one of them will begin to talk about her body. It can crop up during the fellowship time at the women's Bible study, while piling it on at the salad bar, during coffee breaks, or while comparing thigh diameters with your best friend over the phone. You can bet that a woman's opinion of her body will not be complimentary. Women are notorious for hating their bodies.

We're getting worse about this, too. A 1995 study claims that women are even more dissatisfied with their bodies than they were 10 years earlier. In 1985, less than a third (30 percent) of women were dissatisfied with their appearance, while in 1995, nearly half (48 percent) were dissatisfied.[1] And this is after 20 years of excessive media attention to diet, exercise, and general health!

What is body image, what does it have to do with sexuality, and how does any of this fleshly, worldly stuff tie in with God and how He made us?

Good questions. These may not be our most pressing questions each day, but they are important because our answers to them can erode our self-confidence, especially below the conscious level. Most women fall short of full-fledged body hate. But many aren't as fortunate and end up suffering from obsession with their looks (like Joy), anorexia nervosa, bulimia, repetitive cosmetic surgery, or chronic dieting. And who of us hasn't sold unused exercise equipment at garage sales?

What Is Body Image?

Body image is what you think you look like on the outside. Notice I didn't say it's what you look like on the outside. Some of the most beautiful people in the world have the worst body images—and vice versa.

I once worked with a woman who had lost a lot of weight. She would still be considered heavy by the world's standards, but she was proud of having lost the weight she had. She was excited that she could now fit into the fashions for larger women. She had a remarkable talent for coordinating outfits and truly enjoyed it. She also enjoyed her healthier body. No one was beating down her door, asking her to do a fashion-magazine cover, but you would have thought so by the way she saw herself. She finally felt beautiful. Her new clothes made the most of her appearance, and the weight loss was a catalyst to maintain the new her. At the same time she was shedding weight, she was growing closer to God. More important than what was happening to her on the outside was what was going on inside her, something so deep and compelling that it overcame any messages from the world.

This woman had an anchor for her soul. She knew her body was much healthier and that she had achieved a great deal. She was going to be the best woman in the body she had. So if people sneered at her in a bathing suit, they'd better watch out, because she was likely to give them a response that would blow them away.

Then there are the anorexic and bulimic patients I have worked with over the years. In terms of worldly beauty, these women would be considered the gorgeous people, lovely and intelligent. Yet they see themselves as fat and ugly.

As we all know, beauty is in the eye of the beholder. My daughter's reaction to my husband's weight loss is a case in point. While everyone else gave him attention and praise for his new, slim physique, she wasn't impressed. She said that she liked her heavier daddy better. To Rachel, a dad was supposed to be soft and round. She had a different standard for perfection and it took a bit of adjustment for her to get used to his new look.

Body image can also change from moment to moment. I might glance in the mirror and think I look great. Then I look again and realize that I've talked to a dozen people without being aware that I have a piece of lettuce stuck between my teeth, and there goes my body image.

What Is a Healthy Body Image?

My son, Benjamin, who is four at this writing, is an example of someone with a healthy body image. It doesn't faze him at all to run around naked. He is thrilled and amazed by his body. He is constantly discovering the limits of his body's ability to run, jump, and climb. Occasionally, I have to rescue him from the high shelves in the pantry because he can't figure out how to get down.

King David gave us a great example of a healthy body image in Psalm 139. He speaks of being fearfully and wonderfully made. He celebrates the wonder of God as he looks at his own body and recognizes the artwork of a master Creator.

Even more amazing than the fact that our very bodies are the handiwork of God is the incredible truth that God chooses to dwell in them. Second Corinthians 6:16 says that our bodies are the temple of God. That alone is reason enough to treat them with dignity and respect. God could choose anywhere to live. As He cultivated the nation of Israel in preparation for Jesus, He dwelled in a tent-temple. Later He dwelled in the magnificent Temple Solomon built for Him. Today He chooses to dwell in the hearts of the very people who call Him Father. The earthly tabernacle of God is our human bodies.

After actor Christopher Reeve was thrown from a horse and became a quadriplegic, he was interviewed by Barbara Walters. In that interview, he talked about a powerful revelation. He had discovered that he is not his body.[2] Oh, how I long for women to realize this inspirational truth! The time we spend hating the bodies God has given us could be better spent learning to know God and His deep love for us.

Our bodies weren't originally designed to die, but they will because of sin. God promises us new bodies when we get to heaven. In the meantime, God has given us the bodies we have. We need to accept what we look like and believe that God will use us for His glory regardless of the value the world puts on our outside appearance.

A healthy body image combines acceptance of and respect for the body you have been given. It isn't a sense of pride, exactly; it is an agreement that God is the Potter and you are the clay. It is an ability to see beyond the world's message that "you are your body." It is an ability to celebrate that God made you and loves you.

Time for You

Do you think that God made a mistake when He gave you your body?

Do you need to make peace with yourself and accept the parts of your body you cannot change?

How does an unhealthy body image hold you back from what God wants for your life?

Steps to a Healthier Body Image

1. Identify the Parts of Your Body You Hate

Every woman has something that she dislikes about her body. Most women especially despise the area from the waist to the thighs. What bothers you the most about your body?

2. Identify Why You Began to Hate Those Parts

When I talk to parents about helping their children have healthy body images, I often specifically address fathers of adolescent daughters. Many of the women I have counseled who have unhealthy body images have heard words from their fathers during these formative years that have subconsciously stuck with them all their lives. A father's jaded remark cuts deeply into his daughter's sense of value. He might say, "Look at your big hips," or tease her about her bra size, and that does a lot of damage. Other people's comments may also play a major role in why a woman hates her body.

Faye remembered playing tennis with her best friend as a teenager. Some guys stopped by to watch their game. One boy commented to the other, in reference to Faye, "She's too flat." All these years later, those words ring in her head. Fortunately, the ugly words spoken by a stranger didn't prevent Faye from accepting herself as she was. But words do have power. Sometimes abolishing our body hate begins by identifying why we dislike a particular part of our bodies and putting the comments or humiliation that engendered the hatred into perspective.

3. Look at Yourself in Perspective

Since body image is what you think you look like on the outside, developing a healthy body image begins with healthy self-talk. In fact, negative body image is fueled by negative self-talk. This takes many forms. Exaggeration is by far the most common form of unhealthy self-talk that women use. In conversations with other women, we exaggerate our flaws in order to be accepted. We believe the world's philosophy that we *should* all be thin and beautiful. We reject our positive features as we focus on our negative ones. We think others are as obsessed with our flaws as we are.

Judy developed a new body image before she even began to diet and exercise. She believed that she was valuable regardless of her weight. Instead of subconsciously believing that she needed to be overweight to ward off sexual attention, she began to see that her body was her physical home while she lived on earth. She decided to take better care of herself, so she began to diet. She did not equate being thin with being valuable; she already knew her value whether she lost weight or not.

4. Develop an Awareness of Your Positive Features

God has given each of us gifts and talents to build up the body of Christ. Our physical bodies house those talents and gifts. We need to take account of our positive features. Do you have pretty eyes? What is it you like best about the body God gave you?

Women with unhealthy body images focus on one or two flaws even though they may have several attractive characteristics.

5. Change What You Can Change and Accept What You Can't Change

If you don't like certain features about yourself, try to do the best you can with what you have. Use tasteful makeup and clothes to present yourself in a way that makes you comfortable. We do feel better when we are pleased with the way we look. But it is equally important to keep this in balance. An example of this is cosmetic surgery. Many people who have cosmetic surgery feel better about themselves for a short time before again resorting to a negative self-image. The problem isn't with what is wrong on the outside; it's with what is wrong on the inside.

Make the changes that help you deemphasize negative features and emphasize the positive aspects of your body and appearance. The goal is to be free from a preoccupation with your appearance and free to live your life.

6. Keep Growing and Developing Christlikeness

As you grow in your relationship with Christ, life takes on a whole new perspective. The diameter of your thighs somehow fades in importance. Some of the parts of your body that you hate so intensely hardly seem worth the bother. Perhaps there are some you will even be thankful for.

A woman who has an anchor for her soul is not easily tossed about by an overemphasis on her body and appearance.

What Does Body Image Have to Do with Sexuality?

At first I didn't intend to include a chapter on body image or sex. When I was teaching this material to a group of women, many of their questions at the end of our time together helped me see how a discussion of our feminine identity leads us directly to many questions about the physical aspects of femininity. In the world, femininity means sexuality. Our culture insists that the more sex appeal we have, the more feminine we are. That simply is not true.

But that was how Joy lived most of her life, and it left her feeling empty and defeated. Femininity is so much more than how we look and what we wear. But it is difficult for us to embrace our true femininity without discovering a way to look at our bodies as well. They are, as Regina mentioned, the garage for our feminine souls.

Living from the core belief that sexual appeal is what makes a

woman feminine almost cost Joy her life. It was during her involve-
ment in the growth group that Joy first noticed a lump in her
breast. The thought of cancer and a mastectomy completely overwhelmed her. The moment the suspicion entered her mind, she
dismissed it by thinking that she would rather die than lose what
she thought to be so vital to her femininity. She decided to ignore
the lump. But the discussion on bathing suits caught her off guard,
and she revealed her secret. Unanimously, the women insisted that
Joy make an appointment with her doctor the next day. Under that
kind of pressure, she agreed to go.

Joy did have a malignant tumor that required a radical mastectomy to save her life. But she was lucky. Today she is still cancer
free. More important, surviving cancer has taught her a great deal
about sex appeal. She recognized the lie she had believed all of her
life: the idea that she was wanted only for her beauty. She would
never have believed that her husband, Robert, couldn't bear to lose
her or that she meant so much more to him than just an attractive
woman to introduce as his wife to business associates. It opened a
whole new way of seeing herself and her value in the world. She
confessed to Regina several years later that her sex life has become
even more enjoyable since her recovery from cancer. She finally
realized how much her husband treasured her. Sexual experiences
shared in a deeply meaningful relationship just don't compare with
any other kind.

This brings us to the subject of sex. How does God want us to
live our lives in regard to our sexuality?

CHAPTER EIGHTEEN

Celebrating Sexuality God's Way

Sex and the Christian woman seem to be mutually exclusive topics. Although God is not a sexual being, He did create us to be that way. In fact, sex is a metaphor for the key issues we have been talking about. In the sex act, a woman is warm and receiving, while a man must be strong and penetrating. Both the oneness God wants for our relationships and the differences required to create oneness are reflected in the act of intercourse.

The moment sin entered the world, our sexuality underwent enormous changes. In Genesis 2:24–25, Adam and Eve's nakedness produced no shame. But in Genesis 3:7, sexuality instantly became a matter of confusion and fear. For Adam and Eve, the first effect of sin was a desire to hide their sexuality. At some point, we all face a similar sense of shame about our sexuality. No one is immune from this.

For Judy, sex brought shame through the humiliation of sexual abuse. Sharon thought of sex as something a good wife does whether she feels like it or not, and Joy thought sex was for men. Diane felt close through sex, but she feared being completely vulnerable. Brenda, still a virgin, feared that sex might reveal that she was inadequate or unappealing. For Faye, sex brought shame. After having been date-raped in her youth, she felt irrevocably marred. Regina said her worst humiliation from the misuse of sex stemmed from her two abortions. She felt abandoned—left alone to bear the agony while her boyfriends remained footloose and fancy-free.

Obviously, we don't experience our sexuality in the safe cushion of paradise, where it cannot hurt us or others. Because it is a part of how God made us, it is worth our discussion.

How did your parents talk to you about sex? I get some interesting answers to that question. Most people were handed a book and told, "If you have any questions, come and ask me." The message beneath the invitation was, "Please, please don't have any questions, because I'd be horribly embarrassed, and we certainly wouldn't want that, now would we?"

This is how Solomon spoke to his son David about sex. Proverbs 5:18–19 says, "Let your fountain be blessed, and rejoice in the wife of your youth. As a loving hind and a graceful doe, let her breasts satisfy you at all times; be exhilarated always with her love." Even after the fall, God wanted us to celebrate our sexuality. He designed the fullest expression of our sexuality to be experienced in marriage. Sex distinguishes the marriage relationship from all others, because it is in this relationship alone that God desires us to relate sexually with our partner.

Satan has misused our sexuality to lead us down a dangerous and dead-end path that can lead to anything from sexual addictions to complete avoidance of this gift from God. Satan is able to pull off his temptations and deceptions because sex is such a powerful force in our lives. It causes us to buy things, to continue to watch a channel we know we should change, to show poor judgment in a relationship when we know better.

In my work as a marriage counselor, I have been dismayed by the results of misuses of sex and have seen both ends of the spectrum—from an excess to total restraint. I've learned that people who have had more practice and more partners before marriage don't make the best lovers. On the other hand, I've also seen Christians whose puritanical views of sex caused them to enjoy little of the pleasure God wants for them in the marriage bed. Some believe that if they remain virgins, they will have better sex than anyone else in the world because God is required to bless them for their sacrifice. Because of the way God created sex and the differences between men and women, it takes time, patience, and effort to learn how to have great sex.

Sex and the Married Woman

We live in such a sex-craving society that we are often left wondering whether we are missing out on something special because we are Christians. God, our Creator, designed sex for married couples (Gen. 2:24–25), and He designed it to be wonderfully pleasurable (Prov. 5:18–19). The kind of sex the world entices us with focuses on physical pleasure. The kind of sex God speaks about is also pleasurable, but it is so much more than that. Sexual encounters flowing out of a relationship founded on love and commitment enrich and increase emotional as well as physical intimacy.

In the context of a panel discussion, a teenager once asked me, "Are you really suggesting that people have sex with only one person all of their lives? Wouldn't that get boring?" That's an excellent question based on the messages that today's teenagers receive from the world. My answer is that God designed sex to be an enriching part of our journey to intimacy. The kind of sex exploited in the tabloids and talk shows is one thing; the kind of sex God created us to enjoy in a committed, monogamous, and meaningful relationship is quite another. This is especially true for women. For a woman to enjoy and find deeper pleasure in sexual intimacy, she must feel safe in the arms of her lover. That's where the monogamous, committed part comes in. A man is also free to discover the delight of satisfying the wife of his youth when he commits to sex God's way.

Sex can't fix a marriage, and it isn't the center of a good one, but it does help us enjoy marriage more. As we anchor our marriage and commitment to each other in Christ, we find that sexual intimacy is the icing on the cake. In reality, sexual intimacy is good for you. The hormones that are released during sexual intercourse fight depression, help with the immune system, and decrease heart attacks.[1]

When I address audiences at marriage-enrichment seminars, I present six characteristics of good sex for Christian couples. Here they are.

1. Realistic Expectations

If you watch TV or go to movies, you have been exposed to Hollywood's version of good sex. When we compare those experiences with reality, there is often quite a difference. In Hollywood, the sex is always perfect, just like the atmosphere and the people. But in real life, sexual intimacy, like every other endeavor, is not always perfect. Sometimes it will be awkward; sometimes we experience failure; sometimes it is unsatisfying. It is the growth in intimacy that matters.

Many times, women expect their husbands to be fantastic lovers, automatically knowing what pleases them. I tell women they need to take responsibility for their own pleasure during sex. You need to give your husband feedback about what you like. He shouldn't feel that he ought to somehow already know all of this.

If you need help, and most couples do from time to time, don't be afraid to get it. You could begin by checking your Christian bookstore for resources on sexuality and marriage. You could also consult with a Christian marriage counselor.

2. Mutual Consent

Another characteristic of good sex for Christian couples is a sense of mutuality. Many Christian women view sex as something men need and women put up with. Women need sex just as much as men, but they experience the need and the act differently. Because men reach orgasm quickly, neither they nor women always understand and appreciate the difference. Men are capable of having an orgasm within minutes; but after having one, they experience a refactory period (a period of recovery during which further orgasm or ejaculation is physically impossible). Most women require 12 to 14 minutes of stimulation before their bodies are even ready to experience orgasm; but women are able to have multiple orgasms without a refactory period.

Here again is that fundamental difference between men and women, taken to a new dimension. The man's primary pleasure comes in the goal, the end, the achievement. The woman's rests in the extended relationship. And yet it's not a case of either-or. He can take immense pleasure in the long sweetness leading to her orgasm, and she can derive profound satisfaction from pleasing him. Good sex serves a practical purpose in providing for reproduction and the satisfaction of innate needs while giving enjoyment to both partners.

All this means that the couple must be mutually committed to helping each other find pleasure and, of course, mutually consenting to the adventure in the first place. The Christian woman must never forget that God created sex. He created the details of the male and female bodies, not only to make sex pleasurable for men and women, but also to make it necessary that we communicate and discuss our differences so that we can discover how to please each other. Without this complex process, including the quirks in timing, the pleasure for both partners would not be nearly as sublime, nor would it last a lifetime.

Many women feel unfeminine if they initiate sex. Most husbands are very responsive to their wives' invitation because they like it when their wives are also interested in sex. Some women feel uncomfortable admitting they have sexual needs and desires, but God made us to experience them.

3. Romance

There is nothing like a dose of romance to keep a woman interested in marriage. The problem is, men don't usually put the same value on romance. Here is still another aspect of the basic difference between the male and female approach to life. A man's let's-cut-to-the-chase thinking pattern doesn't really need a woman's let's-enjoy-the-process to achieve its end. Often a man doesn't even recognize romance when he sees it. It's not a fault; it's a difference. We women must encourage and sometimes lead in this area. Men aren't opposed to romance. They just don't dwell on it.

I think it's important for a couple to splurge at times (balance is always the key). I challenge couples who don't think weekend getaways, occasional flowers, or a special dinner is worth the money to investigate the price of a divorce these days.

Do you remember when you were dating? What romantic gestures did you make to your spouse then? The funny thing about romance is that after marriage, it begins to feel like work. It took just as much work before marriage, but then it seemed worth it. After all, you were winning your true love. Well, once the marriage bond is in place, both the man and the woman must keep that true love alive.

Do what you can to create romance. Set an example for him by making an extra effort to plan an evening with his special interests. Wear something he likes, light candles, set a special mood for sex. Romance means different things to different men. Learn what pleases your man and plan to make him feel special. Ideally, he will pick up on your gestures and think of ways he could do the same for you.

4. Fidelity

God's plan for our sexuality includes faithfulness to our marriage vows. When we trust God, we believe that His instructions against adultery are in our own best interest. Infidelity sometimes produces physical consequences such as unwanted pregnancy or disease. A woman, incidentally, is more at risk for developing sexually transmitted diseases because these germs thrive in warm, dark, moist places—a perfect description of the vagina. Infidelity always produces emotional consequences, whether the woman or the man is the adulterer. These consequences include depression, anxiety, bitterness, unforgiveness, and guilt.

God wants us to have sex only with our husbands. This doesn't mean sex should be boring. Keep excitement in mind. Sometimes have a quickie; other times let sex be leisurely. Change positions and locations. Read a book written from a Christian perspective such as *The Gift of Sex* by Clifford and Joyce Penner or *Solomon on Sex* by Joseph Dillow.

5. Frequency

I saw a cartoon a long time ago of a couple in the marriage counselor's office. The man is saying to the grumpy-looking woman,

"You see, dear? Lots of couples do it more than once a month." Most people are curious to know if there is a certain number of times per week or month that a couple should have sex, mostly in order to determine if they are doing OK or not. And they're usually disappointed to find out that there is no magic number.

Sex drive (desire expressed in frequency) differs greatly among people. People of nearly identical sex drives hardly ever marry each other. In every marriage, someone is having sex more often than he or she wants, and someone is having sex less often than he or she would like. In good marriages, couples compromise and are able to give and receive in order to satisfy both partners.

6. Communication

When you think of the many profound differences between male and female sexual functions, you might think God made a mistake. The way God designed sex, it is impossible to create a warm and loving union without communication. It's sad to talk to couples who have been married a number of years and still don't know what pleases the other.

Communication is the source of intimacy in marriage, and communication is the foundation for pleasure in the sexual relationship. In order to achieve good sex that is satisfying to both partners, we must communicate. We need to express our likes and dislikes.

Sex and the Single Woman

Sexuality for the single Christian woman is an equally perplexing plight. Though she has no partner with whom to enjoy, explore, and engage her sexual side, she has feelings, urges, and hormones with which to contend.

Single Christian women struggle with their sexuality in different ways. Some are virgins—seeming aliens in today's world. Others may have had sex with one man before being divorced or widowed. Still other single women have had multiple partners.

Our sexuality emphasizes our loneliness. All women struggle with loneliness, but the single woman faces a different kind of loneliness. If she is struggling to trust God's desire that she not engage in sexual encounters outside of marriage, she may feel left out of something important. She is, after all, a sexual being, so when she isn't being sexual, she feels that a part of her isn't even alive.

The grass always seems greener on the other side. I know married women who are experiencing the physical act of intercourse and yet are living with a deadness in their souls. I also know married women who dread the act of sex because of what it represents to them. They may be envious of single women who are not expected to be sexual.

Henri Nouwen wrote: "It is obvious that our brokenness is often most painfully experienced with respect to our sexuality. . . . Our sexuality reveals to us our enormous yearning for communion. The desires of our body—to be touched, embraced and safely held— belong to the deepest longings of the heart and are very concrete signs of our search for oneness."[2]

Intimacy from sexual relationships is only a taste of what our souls are craving. We want to be naked body, mind, and soul and to be completely accepted, embraced, and found pleasurable. Our greatest fear is that nakedness will bring rejection.

Just as we put on clothes to cover our physical nakedness, we put on defenses to cover the nakedness of our minds and souls. We say by our defensive demeanor, "I don't want you to know that you have something I need, lest you keep it from me, and I am left rejected."

Our sexuality alerts us to our need for oneness with another. We will not be able to make ourselves into nonsexual beings.

After her divorce, Diane decided to do without men. For her, sex had not been all that it was cracked up to be. It had been a mistake to marry because she was no good at intimacy. In her words, "The only good things I got from my marriage are these two great kids, and raising them scares me to death. But men, I can do without."

Soon after the divorce, she found herself waking up in the night feeling the urge for sexual pleasure; she hated herself for being so weak and vowed to overcome it. Try as she might, she couldn't completely suppress that part of herself. Like everything else that seemed threatening to Diane, she sought to control it by thinking about something else and ignoring her urges. She determined that sexuality only gets a person into trouble, so she sought to abolish that part of herself, telling herself she needed to be strong. Eventually, she succeeded in repressing her sexual urges. In God's Word, single women are instructed not to have sex without being married. In Diane's case, she was obeying this command, not because of her trust in God, but because she no longer wanted to consider herself a sexual being.

The growth group's discussions about sexuality were helpful to Diane. She confessed to God that her pursuit of nonsexuality had nothing to do with believing His ways are best. Instead, they had everything to do with her need to be in control.

Judy, Diane, and Brenda, each single, asked the group how they should look at themselves as sexual beings. Judy found she needed to trust God that sexuality was good, a special gift He created for her to enjoy in marriage. Because of her childhood experiences, she grew up loathing it. In viewing sex in a new way, she also needed to respect God's instructions about how to behave sexually. In her dating relationships, she set sexual standards for herself that she would not violate. She decided that she would only hug, kiss, and hold hands with a guy to whom she felt a serious commitment.

Brenda shared 1 Thessalonians 4:3–8 with the group. The passage encouraged single women to wait for sex and let true friendship develop with a man. Diane could attest that sex had only clouded her feelings about Tim before they married. She committed to not having sex again unless she was married.

First Corinthians 6:18 says, "Flee immorality. Every other sin that a man commits is outside the body, but the immoral man sins against his own body." It takes just as much grace to cover our sins against our bodies as it does sins committed against others. Sin is sin to God, and grace is the antidote. That grace is possible only because of Jesus' supreme sacrifice—becoming sin for us, so we could receive His grace. Sexual sin hits us hard emotionally in part because it is so personal, by far the most intimate of sins. We carry the effects of that kind of sin with us because it affects our bodies. We can't get away from it because we awaken more desires that seem to overrule our decisions or we are left hurt by sexually transmitted disease, pregnancy, or disrespect. It is difficult to separate sin we've done with our bodies from who we are. That is one of the reasons Diane had such a hard time accepting God's forgiveness after committing adultery.

Sexual Abuse and Sexuality

Because of the prevalence of sexual abuse today, it is important to discuss this issue briefly in a book about femininity. One of the core ways sexual abuse damages women is by creating a deep fear that if one is feminine, pain will surely result.

Many women have been used sexually. There is a difference between what our justice system considers sexual abuse and what our souls consider sexual abuse. As I help women understand their femininity, I broaden the definition of sexual abuse from being touched in sexual areas and forced to have intercourse to include other inappropriate sexual messages and intrusions as well.

For instance, a woman came to counseling because she suspected she had been sexually abused. As she began to talk about her childhood, memories of abuse, including inappropriate sexual behavior, began to surface. She recalled numerous times that her parents' sexual behavior was quite vulgar. She remembered being present while they had sex and being forced to listen to their sexual conversations, which made her feel uncomfortable yet intrigued. Although she could not remember being physically touched by her parents (a legal criterion for sexual abuse), the effect of their inappropriate sexual behavior had a tremendous impact on her psyche. The way her father marched naked around the room after intercourse with her mother gave her the clear message that a woman exists only to be used and conquered by a man.

Another example is a woman I'll call Julie. Nobody ever touched her sexually, but she received a variety of damaging and confusing sexual messages. One confusing message came from the pornography that was prevalent in her home. The images of unclothed women and people involved in sexual acts did not make sense to her young mind, but they certainly made an impression. She saw both her mom and dad regularly reading and viewing this material. Something about it drew her to it, and she struggled with being sexually stimulated while seeing undressed women. For many years she thought she was a lesbian. Julie is an example of a child who has been confused about her sexuality in large part because of her parents' inappropriate behavior.

Anna was never sexually abused as a child, but she had many of the symptoms of those who have been. She suffered recurring nightmares of being chased, and she considered her body and sexuality to be dirty and damaged. In her second marriage, she was submissive to any sexual acts her husband initiated, but she cut herself off from her emotions during them. This was disconcerting to her husband, who desired to bring her pleasure. In therapy, we discovered that these sexual problems probably had their origins in her first marriage. There had been so much trauma in that marriage that she had repressed the fact that her first husband had raped her on several occasions and had abused her emotionally through sexually explicit comments.

There is a correlation in the soul between our sexuality and our identity. The physical sensations resulting from being sexually violated range from feeling nothing to feeling slight pleasure to feeling pain. All do damage. If the woman feels pleasure, she invariably feels guilty and may even think she caused the abuse. If a woman feels nothing, it is because she has disassociated from her body—which is not good in itself—and she also feels she is wrong. If she experiences pain, it is because the perpetrator is hurting her body. But the greater damage is done to the emotions.

Emotionally, the woman feels sick, used, and dirty. She develops a core belief that something about her is wrong and that is why this is happening. Many times she takes these bad feelings out on her body. Her body is the closest she can get to the scene of the crime. She might gain a lot of weight as a way to avoid relationships with men. She might become bulimic or anorexic. She may feel suicidal and depressed because she represses her anger and feelings of disgust for fear of experiencing even greater pain and rejection.

The greatest damage she can do is to cut herself off from her soul. In effect, she commits emotional suicide, thinking if she lets herself feel at all, it will only bring pain. In this way she becomes disconnected from her love needs, and that in turn disconnects her from God and others.

That is how Judy lived for a number of years. As she recovered from sexual abuse, she got back in touch with her body. She realized that her weight was her god, her way of protecting herself from men. (In fact, people in psychotherapy usually refer to obesity as "the fat pad" or "the fat shield.") She began a diet and exercise program and slowly took off the weight. She finally discovered it was safe to be a woman. Judy committed herself to living according to God's plan for her and not as a victim.

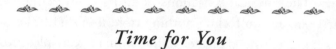

Time for You

How do you feel about your body and your sexuality?

Do you trust God's plan for your sexuality?

Femininity, Sexuality, and God

How we view our bodies and our sexuality says a lot about our trust in God. Do you trust that God made you? I think we should each wear one of those tags that sometimes come on garments or handbags: "The material used to manufacture this garment is uniquely designed. Any flaws that appear are part of the unique quality and are not considered flaws in the material." Do you trust God that the full expression of your sexuality should be reserved for a monogamous, committed, married relationship? He tells you that only because He loves you. Learn to trust the God who made you. Accept the feminine physique He gave you. Rejoice in being the temple of the Holy Spirit. Treat yourself with respect and dignity.

CHAPTER NINETEEN

A Woman After God's Own Heart

Little girls begin planning their weddings as young children. They think about the dresses they will wear. They talk about the appearance of the groom. They look to marriage as a kind of redemption. After all, once Snow White and Cinderella found their princes and were married, everyone lived happily ever after. The only reality that can spoil that little-girl notion is a couple of years of marriage itself. Planning a wedding requires a lot of work, but marriage requires even more.

There is another wedding feast to which we can look forward. It is a wedding in which we are not only the person being honored but also the invited guest. We are invited to be the bride of Christ. But being the bride of Christ does not require all the work and effort asked of a bride on earth. We are invited to the wedding feast of the Lamb. All that needs to be done has been done for us.

My mother made my wedding dress. It was beautiful and took hours to complete. As the bride of Christ, our wedding dress is taken care of by the Groom. We will wear His robes of righteousness, woven for us by His sacrificial gift, His own life. We women (and men) often don't realize what is promised to us. There will be a point in time that God will be able to love us as completely as He desires. He will bring us, the church, to Christ, our Groom.

With the divorce rate on the rise and love for a lifetime being seen as an outdated notion, the full beauty of the metaphor of a wedding and God's love for us is obscured. On earth, a wedding is the hope of all hopes. We are each hoping to find the relationship that will heal us, that will complete us. We are all hoping that we will discover the one person who will love us unconditionally. But whether we ever marry on earth or not, there is a Groom who is waiting patiently to celebrate His love for us the way He desires. Before Jesus left this earth, He instituted the sacrament of the wine and bread. He told the disciples then that He would not eat of the wine and bread until we are reunited with Him in heaven (Luke 22:15–16). He is a Groomsman greater than all groomsmen, the true love of our lives; and best of all, He is willing to wait for us.

If you are like me, you are eager for that wedding feast to take place. You long to be loved the way you were created to be loved, with no obstacles or misunderstandings. In my anticipation for that wedding to take place, I've noticed something. It is the patience of the Groom. Generation after generation passes on this earth, and still our Groom waits for His special celebration. Brian and I were engaged for eight months, and that seemed an eternity. Jesus has been waiting nearly 2,000 years. Why is He so patient?

Several things are clear. One is that Jesus loves us. The second is that God has a plan. God lets us know about the wedding feast, but the day and hour it will occur are not for us to know, and He is clear about that, too (Matt. 24:36). God tells us how He wants to love us then, when there are no barriers of sin, so that we will desire to respond to His love now.

Some of the most memorable moments of my marriage to Brian were the seminary days. We were broke. Going out to Arby's was a big deal. We lived in a little, run-down apartment with a couch we bought for $25. Remembering those days, I realize that we laid a strong foundation for our marriage then because all we had was each other. We weren't distracted by material possessions or children. Those years were wonderful for building love and intimacy between us.

I think of my years on earth as an opportunity to discover the love of God in a unique way. I know He loves me, and I know what He has planned for me. But it seems that He also has given me these years on earth to discover His love even in uncomfortable living conditions. Might this be like our earthly marriages? I know couples who begin their marriages having it all. The bride has a Jaguar in the driveway, takes fabulous trips, and owns a beautiful home. None of it guarantees a good marriage. You cannot buy happiness. It is a gift. If God gave me everything I wanted instantly, He couldn't teach me about what I really want.

Discovering God's love here on earth must only make my experience of meeting Him face to face more meaningful. God doesn't just want me to know how much He loves me. He also yearns for me to love Him back. On some level, that yearning might seem as though we serve a greedy and self-centered God. The Westminster Catechism says that the chief end of man is to glorify God and enjoy Him forever.

When I think about this, I see how glorifying God saves me from myself. I realize that if I am not glorifying God, I am glorifying myself. When I glorify myself, I often hurt others in the process. I don't accomplish the desires in my soul to love and be loved. This world was created to be in balance. It is only when God is in His rightful place as the center of our lives that we can live in balance. God rescues me from existing to glorify myself because this position damages me. It is only as we seek to glorify God that unity is established within ourselves, with others, and with God.

My hope for my life on earth is to become a woman after God's own heart. I want to respond to His love and to experience as much of it as I can while I live here. What does it mean to be a woman after God's own heart?

A Woman After God's Own Heart Accepts God's Purposes

For as long as I've been alive, I've struggled to get my way. As a baby, I wanted to be fed when I was hungry, to be changed when I was wet, to be held when I was lonely, and to wake and sleep on my own timetable. Babies are resolute about demanding this kind of attention because that is the only way they know how to survive. As a baby Christian, I still want my own way. I want to be comfortable. I want lots of money, nice clothes, a nice house, and a nice car. I think of ways to make myself more comfortable on a daily basis.

As a growing Christian, I have discovered the battle within regarding releasing my desire to get my own way and accepting whatever God would have for me. Jesus is a perfect example of following the way of the Father. T. W. Hunt, a Christian writer, said, "Jesus' entire motivation was to advance those causes which cannot be measured physically or materially. These causes can be perceived only by spiritually sensitive persons."[1] Jesus showed us a way of living this life, focused not on earthly comforts but on comfort for our souls. He came with a mission, and that mission was to do the will of the Father. Ephesians 5 says:

> Watch what God does, and then you do it, like children who learn proper behavior from their parents. Mostly what

God does is love you. Keep company with him and learn a life of love. Observe how Christ loved us. His love was not cautious but extravagant. He didn't love in order to get something from us but to give everything of himself to us. Love like that. *(The Message)*

God's way is not that of a tyrant, demanding power and control. His way is that of love, always inviting us to ever-deepening intimacy. But we choose to go our own way. When we try to love our way—loving to get and loving to control—we end up loveless. One of the signs of the end times that Jesus mentioned is lovelessness. He said, "And because lawlessness is increased, most people's love (agape) will grow cold" (Matt. 24:12). Our souls are created for love, but this love can't exist without God, or it will be selfish and demanding. We must exchange our own way for God's way.

A Woman After God's Own Heart Is Spiritually Sensitive

Philippians 3 says, "So let's keep focused on that goal, those of us who want everything God has for us. If any of you have something else in mind, something less than total commitment, God will clear your blurred vision—you'll see it yet! Now that we're on the right track, let's stay on it" *(The Message)*.

I would never want to be one of those who reduces God to a tiny voice inside of me. Our God is much greater than that. But our God is one who gives us messages of His love and His righteousness daily. He speaks to us in a still, small voice. We must learn to be spiritually sensitive so we can recognize it.

A friend asked me how I hear God speaking to me. When I tune in to God, I hear His messages deep in my heart while reading the Bible, discipling my kids, driving my car, listening to the radio. It is not an audible voice, but the message my heart receives is clear to me. Sometimes I hear His voice, and I choose not to obey; then I am grieved by the end results—for example, when I ignore the voice that tells me to apologize for what I've done wrong in my relationship with Brian.

It takes a lot of discipline to sincerely listen to God's voice. It is easy to miss what He has to say to me because He doesn't grab me by the shoulders and shake me. His patience with me is beyond understanding. If I were He, I would have given up on me long ago. When I ignore His voice again and again, I wonder why He keeps trying to get through to me. But once again, thank God I'm not God. He is so good, so patient, and so loving that He doesn't stop calling me by name and telling me about Himself and our relationship and what life is all about. And so far He keeps doing it in that gentle voice.

God's voice is the one that exposes my sin yet always invites me to greatness. If you are listening to a voice that describes your failures again and again and you think it is God's voice, you aren't hearing God.

God exposes my sin to me only in increments. God teaches us about our sin in the same way we teach our children a new skill such as walking. First we encourage them as they crawl. Then we praise them for standing and cruising along the couch. Next we let them hold our hands as they learn to walk. Then one day they take off on their own.

When at 16 I began listening to God's voice in a deeper way, the first thing He showed me to change was my rebellious behavior. Today I'm not involved in any sins that would be obvious to you. But there are sins deep in my heart that God shows me because they keep me from the best He wants me to experience. Every stage of showing me my sin has flowed from His kindness. He doesn't show me everything at once. If I knew at 16 that I not only had to stop my rebellious behavior but that I also had to attend to all these other matters, I would probably have given up. It would have been much easier to be wild than to follow God.

We know we are hearing God's voice when it is not accusing. He convicts us of sin only because He longs for us to do better. While I was in labor with my first child and had reached the pushing stage, it was my doctor who called me to my potential. When the nurse first asked me to push, the doctor had not yet entered the room. I pushed, but not too hard. For one thing, there wasn't anyone there to catch the baby! When the doctor came in, she watched me push and said, "You can do better than that." On the next push, out came Rachel. God knows our abilities because He knows how we are made and He knows the power available to us through Jesus Christ to overcome sin. He wants us to experience the best. That's why He convicts us of sin. But He never uses harassment or discouragement to get His message across.

There are myriad voices entering our heads every day. Only we can decide which voices to be sensitive to. Brenda told the story of inviting a friend out to dinner along with a group of people. She thought she felt God speaking to her about paying for her friend's meal, but she made no arrangements to do this. She ignored the Holy Spirit's leading. The friend did come to the meal, but she made up a story about having just eaten and ordered coffee. Brenda felt awful for ignoring God's voice. It crushed her to know that she could have made that evening much more enjoyable for her friend if she had listened to God.

God doesn't shout at us; He whispers our names. Do you hear Him? Do you sense Him calling you away from the world and the false hopes it gives us?

A Woman After God's Own Heart Is Focused on Loving Others

Much of Jesus' message to His disciples the night before He was crucified was about loving one another (John 13–17). His last prayer for us was that we would give and receive love. The message of the gospel is the message of God's great love for us. A true disciple of Christ will be transformed from living a life of self into living a life of love.

This, too, is opposite human nature. If you were to observe my life to discover whom I love most, it would still be myself. I even have to make a constant effort to put my children's needs before my own. I remember being stuck in a hotel room with my son and daughter, waiting for the pool to open so I could take them swimming. To be honest, they were getting on my nerves. As I began to write in my journal and talk to God amid their fighting and the blaring of the TV, I took the time to ask Jesus how He would parent these children. My irritability was challenged when I thought of Jesus. This is what I wrote:

> I'm at the [hotel] with the kids, waiting until we can swim. The kids are driving me slightly crazy, yet I got really mad at Brian last night for being so irritable with them. Here I feel just like him. How would Jesus parent these two?
>
> I think He would have a smile on His face most of the time. I think He would hold them and laugh with them and talk to them. I'm thinking of reading my Bible and painting my nails. Jesus did take time to be alone with God like I am now—but as quickly as He was able, He came back to His followers to live out the lessons He wanted to teach them.

After thinking about Jesus that way, I decided I could paint my nails later and focused on loving my kids instead.

Do you resemble God by the way that you love? Do others know you are a Christian by the love you show in your life? Jesus says that other people should be able to recognize us as Christians by the evidence of our love for others (John 13:35). I am humbled by my lack of love even as I drive down the highway. In Dallas, I do a lot of driving. I feel as if I'm in competition with people to be the first in a lane, to make it through the yellow light, to find the lane that is moving the fastest. In the process, there is no love in my heart. I'm insulted by the guy who pulls into the insufficient space I left between me and the car in front so as to discourage cutters. When he pulls in anyway and I have to touch my brakes, I'm shocked at the hate seeping from my heart. Here I am, hating a person I don't even know, to whom I've never spoken, but who has delayed me just a little in getting to my destination.

God doesn't want me to be a petty driver, risking my life for a chance to be first. He wants so much more for me. He knows I can do better than that. He wants me to be like Him, to learn the freedom of loving others when there is no reason to love. Jesus had the audacity to instruct His disciples to love even their enemies (Matt. 5:44). Imagine that! Loving enemies!

Sometimes I even find it hard to share two inches on an airplane.

One hot afternoon, on a flight taking off from Miami, I ended up sitting next to a rather large man, who was sweating profusely in the heat. He had turned my air conditioner on himself before I arrived at my window seat. I didn't mind the air conditioner, but the elbow jutting past the armrest into the back of my seat really bugged me. I have a thing about my space on airplanes;

just ask my husband. I get this attitude. This seat is mine and that's yours. We should split the armrest right down the middle. Why was it so hard for me to share? Is it because I felt I was being taken advantage of?

Jesus said, "Whoever hits you on the cheek, offer him the other also; and whoever takes away your coat, do not withhold your shirt from him either" (Luke 6:29). Is this the kind of situation Jesus was talking about? The man sitting next to me was a stranger; he didn't even know I was a Christian; he hadn't bothered to ask about my life. As I overheard his conversations, I realized his entire family was sitting together in the three seats across the aisle. It appeared that none of them wanted to sit by him.

Why can't I be sitting next to his petite teenage daughter? I thought. *Why should I give in to him? Will it help him grow as a person? Most likely, it won't.*

Who would be the beneficiary of such a love? At first I thought it would be the man with the extra two inches and the air conditioner pointing his way. When I thought a little harder, I realized that when I love like that, I love like Jesus! I begin to resemble God again. I'm no longer angry when I choose to love. I'm free to give my two inches because they are mine and he is large and I have room in my heart to share.

The real test will come when it's my own husband taking up the two inches. Will I love Brian enough to give up my two inches without demanding my space? It's easier to bother my own husband than it is a stranger.

This life of love is only possible by getting in touch with the One who truly loves us. The closer I get to God's heart, the more I want to love others. I long to love because I have been so deeply loved.

A Woman After God's Own Heart
Finds Comfort in God

If there is one drive that keeps me from being sensitive to God and from living a life of love, it is my commitment to my own comforts. Since the time of Eve, we have been forced to live in a world that seems bent on denying us what we want. Think of a baby leaving her mother's womb and hitting the harsh reality of light, cold, wet diapers, and hunger. Babies cry because they are uncomfortable. Parents' and caregivers' jobs are to figure out where the discomfort is coming from and to make it better. Some of us never grow out of seeking our own comfort. In fact, it is a spiritual battle to be content in spite of discomfort and to find that even pain can lead to joy.

I went to the dentist because I had a toothache and wanted to get rid of the pain. I discovered that I had to endure more pain before I could receive relief. I had to endure the pain of the cure before I could enjoy the results.

Isn't that what Christ did on the cross? Hebrews 12:2 says that for the joy set before Him, He endured the shame and the discomfort of the cross. Think about the degree of discomfort Jesus endured for us, not only on the cross but during His life on earth. For most of us, the discomfort we endured during infancy compares little with the pain we felt in childhood and adulthood. But consider being God and becoming human. It would be similar to you or me taking on the form of a cockroach. For God, just being human was uncomfortable.

When I read the psalms, I am amazed by David's willingness to receive God's comfort. He described situations much worse than I've ever had to endure. He spoke of being homeless, hungry, beaten up, and forsaken. But by the end of every psalm, he had

270 Then God Created Woman

received comfort. The comfort he received didn't come from a change in circumstances. In many of those psalms, David was being pursued by enemies who were trying to kill him, and he was still hiding out in caves and living like a madman. But he received comfort from God, who was always near.

Jesus tells us that if we want to come after Him, we are to take up our crosses and follow Him. I often ask God what it really means to take up my cross. I don't believe I have grasped the full impact of this statement, but I do believe that a great part of it involves abandoning our pursuit of comfort.

I'm not very old, but I'm already beginning to experience some effects of aging—those little aches and pains, the way a day of physical play with the kids can send me to a hot bath to soak. In our culture, we do not tolerate discomfort well. Industries in our society make billions of dollars from our pursuit of comfort.

We need to accept suffering and poverty as a pathway to joy. It's not that we shouldn't take an aspirin when we have a headache, but we could give up that urge to buy a spring wardrobe and give the money to others with more pressing needs.

Pursuing our physical comforts will prevent us from experiencing the comforts that God longs to give us. God's comforts are peace and contentment, which are far more valuable than anything money can buy.

A Woman After God's Own Heart Communicates Soul to Soul with God

I remember sitting in church one day listening to our pastor describe the sermons he was planning to preach in the coming weeks. One of the sermons would deal with the subject of prayer. As he spoke, I was struck with the idea of writing a book about prayer.

After all, I thought, *so many people I know really don't know how to pray. Such a book would be a best-seller.*

I hadn't pursued that thought far before I began to laugh at myself. What did I really know about prayer?

In my journey to learn more about prayer, I have discovered how multifaceted it is. Prayer is a dialogue between a person and God. Prayer transforms us in a way that other dialogues do not. Prayer is as simple as talking to a friend and as awesome as being heard at the very throne of heaven.

I love this description of prayer:

> The important thing about prayer is that it is almost inde-finable. You see, it is: hard and sharp, soft and loving, deep and inexpressible, shallow and repetitious, a groaning and a sighing.
>
> A silence and a shouting, a burst of praise digging deep down into loneliness, into me. Loving. Abandonment to despair, a soaring to heights which can be only ecstasy, dull plodding in the greyness of mediocre being—laziness, boredom, resentment.
>
> Questing and questioning, calm reflection, meditation, cogitation. A surprise at sudden joy, a shaft of light, a laser beam. Irritation at not understanding, impatience, pain of mind and body hardly uttered or deeply anguished.
>
> Being together, the stirring of love shallow, then deeper, then deepest. A breathless involvement, a meeting, a long-ing, a loving, an inpouring.[2]

A woman after God's own heart grows in her conversation with God. Since I realized what I didn't know about prayer, God has shown me a great deal. The more I learn about prayer, the less I understand it. I can tell you one thing for sure, though: It works.

Think about what happens when we pray. Father, Son, and Holy Spirit are all involved in conversation with us! Romans 8:34 says that Jesus Christ is sitting at the right hand of God interceding for us. We pray, and Jesus Himself tells God about us. Romans 8:26 says that the Holy Spirit also intercedes on our behalf, putting into words the thoughts and ideas that are too deep for us to understand or express. And then there is this magnificent description of God in Isaiah 6:1: "I saw the Lord seated on a throne, high and exalted, and the train of his robe filled the temple" (NIV). Oh, the utter power of God!

Though the very act of prayer remains mysterious to me, I can testify that it transforms my personality. It changes me from being self-centered, worried, and preoccupied to being loving, at peace, and centered. I have seen prayer do the same for others. I have witnessed prayer overcome anxiety, depression, despair, and desperation in the lives of people I counsel. Prayer changes the deepest gauges of our souls and somehow aligns them again so that our souls are free to know God's love.

A Woman After God's Own Heart Is Deeply Assured of God's Love for Her

A woman who is close to the heart of God knows there is no other being who loves her more than God Himself. Like Mary of Bethany, who made eye contact with Jesus while He lived here on earth, and Mary Ellen, who made heart contact with Him, we can each come to know His great love.

The world of contemporary Christian music expresses these truths well to me. "His Stubborn Love" and "He's Dying to Reach You" are genuine love songs. When you realize that nothing can separate you from God's love, you know the most important truth that holds your life and, in fact, the entire universe together.

When my kids squabble, I am often summoned to the room.

One may have said wrong words to the other or hit, pushed, or kicked the other. I remind the one, "Benjamin is God's son, and it is wrong for you to treat God's son that way." Or another time, I might say, "Rachel is my daughter. You should not call my daughter a name like that." Those words seem to get their attention. The value of their sibling is put into perspective.

This method works both ways. One day when I was yelling at Rachel for something she had done, she said to me, "I am God's daughter, and you shouldn't talk to God's daughter like that."

I said, "You know, you are right."

I'm glad she's getting the picture. A woman after God's own heart knows whose daughter she is. She doesn't mistreat herself or let others mistreat her. She realizes that she is special.

A Woman After God's Own Heart Changes Her World

Oliver Wendell Holmes said, "I find the greatest thing in this world is not so much where we stand as in what direction we are moving."[3] In what direction are you moving? Are you making a difference in the world? Some people are remembered for generations. Perhaps they founded a nation, painted a masterpiece, or were the first to walk on the moon. The vast majority of us, though, will wither like the grass and go unremembered after we die. But we are each given 70 to 80 years, God willing, to make a difference in the lives of the people with whom we share our planet.

God says that the sins of our fathers are visited on succeeding generations. So, although we may not be remembered, how we live will affect those who come after us. How will you live your life on earth? Will you make a spiritual difference? Or will you commit sins that will affect generations to come? Our goal should be to leave this world a better place by virtue of the spiritual heritage we leave behind.

Women Grasp
Their True Identity

Judy, Sharon, Joy, Diane, Brenda, Faye, and Regina
shared their lives with us. All made major steps in their
spiritual growth by revealing themselves and finding God
in a truer, deeper way. After meeting together for six
months, they met for a final time. Each looked around
the room and saw the faces of women who had touched
her life in long-lasting ways. Each had grown in how she
viewed the others and in how she looked at the world.

As Regina surveyed the members of the group, she had
tears in her eyes. "I feel like a proud mother as I look
around this room."

She told each woman how much she had grown and
encouraged her to continue her journey toward deeper joy
and knowledge of Jesus.

After Regina spoke, everyone exploded with praise and
delight. You would never have guessed that such a diverse
group of women would have so much in common and so
much love for one another.

What did Regina say to each of these women?

Regina told Judy how pleased she was to see her taking

responsibility for her life. Regina noted that Judy had asked for a raise at the bookstore where she had worked for four years. She commented on Judy's courage to stay with her diet, even though it opened the door to being attractive to men. She reminded her that she was proud of her for accepting that date and encouraged her to continue to seek God's best.

Judy agreed. "All my life, I've been expecting trouble. I think being in this group and being focused on discovering God's love have changed me. I'm not so pessimistic. Shedding that bitterness is so freeing." Knowing that these caring women wouldn't want her to be complacent, she added hastily, "But I will be careful. I know that there is a lot of bad out there. It's just that now I don't think that I'm the one who deserves it. I'll protect myself, but I won't go around expecting it anymore."

Sharon's heart was touched by Judy's response. Sharon had viewed Judy as unimportant and doomed to failure because she wouldn't take charge of her life. Now Sharon realized that she envied Judy a little. Judy didn't struggle with having to run everything as Sharon did. Most of all, Sharon felt a love for Judy that didn't come from anything Judy had done for her. It was simply a love for a fellow sister in Christ. Sharon spontaneously hugged Judy and told her that if she ever needed a "mom," she would be there for her.

At that, Regina turned her attention to Sharon. "You've always been a woman I could count on. Now you're a woman I can talk to. Before you were good at getting things done. Now there is no one in this group who has encouraged me more. I guess it's been your view of Jesus. It's obvious to all of us that ever since that night Mary Ellen spoke to us, you've been trying to really know Jesus. Yet you are going about it in a totally different way from your old self. You're being still and letting Jesus reveal Himself to you in His way and on His terms instead of trying to tell God what He ought to do for you. You are truly a testimony to the power of Jesus. I've got to be honest with you—I hesitated to invite you to this group. I didn't think it was possible to break through your walls of anger. But nothing has been more inspirational than to see you change. Thank you for coming and opening your heart to us. I'm excited to hear how God is using you to encourage other mothers in your eating disorders support group. It's nice to see you in church, receiving God's Word and worshiping Him, rather than being in charge of the ladies' craft fair."

Diane piped up to sing Sharon's praises. She pointed out what learning about Sharon's marriage had meant to her. She had originally thought that someone like Sharon had good reasons to get a divorce. Sharon's commitment to go back to Ed and try to make her marriage work would spur Diane to try harder, when and if she ever married again, to obey God even when times got rough. Since Tim had remarried, she was going to take time to find God's will for her life. She ended by saying, "I'm going to give up control and trust God to do with me what He sees best, and that includes marriage."

Regina smiled. "Diane, I think I grieved for you most of all. I hated to hear that you had so little nurturing in your early years. No kid deserves that. So I'm especially pleased that you've allowed the women here to nurture you. I hope that you, more than anyone else here, will stay closely connected with the rest of us."

Regina then described for the group a scene she had not mentioned before. She said she knew for sure that Diane was "getting it" the Sunday she overheard her talking to her six-year-old after choir. Andy had skinned his knee and was whimpering. Diane stopped, found a tissue, sat beside him, and empathized with his pain. Others were carrying on with their business, but at that moment Diane was in the process of reversing something tragic that had begun in her own childhood. She was nurturing her son and nurturing herself at the same time. She was allowing that special part of her feminine nature to approach the moment with compassion and care, even though her head may have been saying, "We need to keep moving. He's a boy. He needs to learn to get over it."

Brenda's eyes grew wet as Regina talked about Diane and her children. There was nothing Brenda wanted more than to have a husband and family. She longed to have opportunities to nurture.

Regina noticed the tears and said to Brenda, "You've come so far to be willing to look at men differently. I'm so glad you won't completely miss the opportunity to see that not all men are mean and cruel and that their perspectives do help make this world a better place. There is nothing that we as a group wish more for you than a husband and family. In the meantime, I'm glad to see you out there, being what God would have you be right now. You aren't waiting for a husband to begin your life. The time you spend being a Big Sister is a great service to the community and in many ways to yourself as well, because you have learned that in giving you receive much more."

Faye told Brenda how helpful it was to see service placed in proper balance. She told Brenda that they both shared the same desire to love and care for others, but Brenda hadn't let that become her identity. Faye warned her not to do that.

Regina decided it was time to address her comments to Faye. "You showed us the courage you've always had beneath your sweet smile. It was wonderful to see you admit that you were angry, hard as it must have been for you. It was even more wonderful to see you get a handle on your life. You are finding balance, too. I'm pleased that your servanthood is an expression of your real love for

Jesus and not simply the outgrowth of some psychological need."

True to her name, Joy's comments were uplifting. She spoke from her heart. "Faye, I can't tell you how much our friendship means to me. It's so honest! I hope that we can continue in it."

Regina fought back tears as she talked to Joy. "It hurts me to think that you could be in big trouble right now if you had not gone to the doctor to find out about your cancer. There's nothing that I've enjoyed more than seeing you become a real person, whether that meant you were angry or happy. It feels good to talk to someone who is, rather than someone who is trying to be."

Regina kept to herself her best memory of Joy's growth. It was the day they had met for lunch at the country club. Joy arrived wearing a pair of shorts and a sports shirt just because that was what she happened to be wearing when they had decided to go out. Regina knew then that Joy had come a long way.

Each of these women had discovered new truths about God and herself. Each had taken difficult steps to act on her discoveries. Each had learned where she fit in the world and had discovered unique ways to show God's love.

That's how God longs for us to live in this world. He wants us to know who we are, who we were born to be, and how to enjoy the gift of the life He has given us.

Living for Jesus will mean swimming against the world's current. We may not find approval from our society. But so what?

We are the nurturers and helpers, the thinkers and peacemakers. We do, and we make do. We bask in His love.

He made us and we are His. There is nothing like us!

$\mathcal{N}$otes

Introduction

1. Saint Augustine, *The Confessions of St. Augustine,* Christian Classics in Modern English (Wheaton, Ill.: Harold Shaw, 1991), p. 235.

Chapter 3

1. OxFam American, UN Population Fund, United States Agency for International Development. Quoted in *EMC Today* (Feb./Mar. 1993): 12.

2. James C. Dobson, *Love for a Lifetime* (Portland, Ore.: Multnomah Press, 1987), pp. 42–43.

3. Anne Moir and David Jessel, *Brain Sex* (New York: Laurel, 1989), p. 17.

4. Ibid., p. 19.

5. Susan Moore, "Women and Sports," *Congressional Quarterly,* 2, 9 (1992): 195–211.

6. Bill Marvel, "Honestly, Are Women More Moral?" *Dallas Morning News,* May 16, 1991.

7. Carol Gilligan, *In a Different Voice* (Cambridge, Mass.: Harvard University Press, 1982), p. 8.

8. Ronda DeSola Chervin, *Prayers of the Women Mystics* (Ann Arbor: Servant Publications, 1992), p. 77.

9. Ruth Senter, *Longing for Love* (Colorado Springs, Colo.: NavPress, 1991), p. 13.

Chapter 4

1. Elizabeth Cady Stanton, *The Original Feminist Attack on the Bible* (New York: Arno Press, 1974), p. 27.

2. Larry Crabb, *Finding God* (Grand Rapids: Zondervan, 1993), p. 86.

Chapter 6

1. Max Lucado, *A Gentle Thunder* (Dallas: Word, 1995), p. 47.

2. Erma Bombeck, *Forever, Erma* (Kansas City, Mo.: Andrews & McMeel, 1996), p. 123.

3. This quotation is taken from *The Love of God* by Oswald Chambers, copyright © 1985 by Oswald Chambers Publications Assn., Ltd., and is used by permission of Discovery House Publishers, Box 3566, Grand Rapids, MI 49501. All rights reserved.

Chapter 9

1. Henry Drummond, *The Changed Life* (Titusville, Fla.: Soul Care Inc., 1988), p. 31.

Chapter 10

1. Oswald Chambers, *My Utmost for His Highest* (Grand Rapids: Discovery House, 1992), March 19.

2. Henri Nouwen, *Life of the Beloved* (New York: Crossroad, 1992), p. 28.

Chapter 11

1. Henri Nouwen, *The Return of the Prodigal Son* (New York: Doubleday, 1992), p. 37.

2. Louis Evely, *That Man Is You* (New York: Paulist Press, 1967), p. 72.

3. Henry Drummond, *The Greatest Thing in the World* (Uhrichsville, Ohio: Barbour, 1994), p. 99.

Chapter 12

1. Walter Wangerin, *As for Me and My House* (Nashville: Thomas Nelson, 1987), p. 79.

2. C. S. Lewis, ed., *George MacDonald: An Anthology* (London: Geoffrey Bles, 1970), p. 26.

3. Walter A. Henrichsen, *Disciples Are Made, Not Born* (Wheaton, Ill.: Victor, 1978), p. 16.

Chapter 13

1. Martin Luther, "Preface," *The Complete Edition of Luther's Latin Writings* (St. Louis: Concordia, 1972), 34:336–337.

Chapter 14

1. Tim Kimmel, *Powerful Personalities* (Colorado Springs, Colo.: Focus on the Family, 1993), p. 75.

Chapter 15

1. Harriet Braiker, *The Type E Woman* (Chicago: Signet, 1986), p. ix.

2. Anne Moir and David Jessel, *Brain Sex* (New York: Laurel, 1989), p. 100.

3. Henry Drummond, *The Changed Life* (Titusville, Fla.: Soul Care Inc., 1988), p. 35.

4. Henri Nouwen, *Here and Now* (New York: Crossroad, 1994), p. 77.

Chapter 16

1. James C. Dobson, Newsletter from Focus on the Family, February 1995.

2. Gary Smalley and John Trent, *The Hidden Value of a Man* (Colorado Springs, Colo.: Focus on the Family, 1992), p. 91.

3. *Dallas Morning News,* Feb. 15, 1993, n.p.

4. "Household Arrest," *Dallas Morning News,* Feb. 17, 1993, n.p.

5. "Love and Life Spans: Marriage Favors Men But Not Women, Study Finds," *Dallas Morning News,* Mar. 23, 1992, n.p.

6. Thomas à Kempis, *The Imitation of Christ,* Christian Classics in Modern English (Wheaton, Ill.: Harold Shaw, 1991), pp. 118–119.

Chapter 17

1. Nanci Hellmich, "Looking Thin and Fit Weighs More on Women," *USA Today,* Sept. 25, 1995.

2. ABC News, *20/20* Transcript #1539, p. 5.

Chapter 18

1. Kristin Von Kreister, "The Healing Powers of Sex," *Reader's Digest* (June 1993): 17–20.

2. Henri Nouwen, *Life of the Beloved* (New York: Crossroad, 1992), p. 73.

Chapter 19

1. T. W. Hunt, *The Mind of Christ* (Nashville: Lifeway Press, 1995), p. 146.

2. From the poem "It's Me, O Lord," by Michael Hollings and Etta Gullick. Reprinted by permission.

3. Oliver Wendell Holmes, cited in *Guideposts* (Aug. 1996): 62.